D1461516

The Barbed Wire Fence

by Arno Christiansen

New Generation Publishing

Prologue

This is not intended as a treatise on the futility of war, because that has been done before by much cleverer people. Neither is it a stirring story of escape, patriotism and bravery, because that too has been done before, by people much better qualified to write about it.

This is a perfectly straightforward and true story, of an ordinary young German; at least in so far as any one human being can be called 'ordinary'. Not particularly concerned about, nor interested in politics, but subscribing to the currently held idealised image of the Führer, he was called upon to fight for his country, for the Third Reich, and willingly did so.

He was captured in the autumn of 1944, and became a prisoner of war in England. This is the story of his captivity, a light-hearted view. Sometimes a little sad, but often funny. This is about ingenuity in adversity, and how the fatalist more often than not survives all others.

A German Soldier and Prisoner of War in England
1944-1948

A very dedicated young German – Herbert could be any one of millions who have ever fought a war. At the beginning he is full of eager energy, believing in everything and everyone and slowly but surely having that belief torn and beaten from his body. Hunger that creeps up on him slowly until it's briefly abated by the eternal bully beef and a chunk of white bread. The reader is compelled to feel all of Herbert's emotions one by one but at the same time feeling the underlying strength of character that pulls him through these four painful years.

None of these times could be called 'good times' but Herbert remembers the amusing and sometimes downright silly things that his fellow POWs and he would get up to, just to pass a few hours or minutes.

Altogether a most compelling book, often very funny but with an underlying current of sadness that makes someone who has never been through any of it – wonder how the hell they did it!

Chapter I:

France, 1944

'I wish those silly fools would understand that this bleeding tank had been abandoned.' Herbert Baum-Hacker once more ground his face into the soft mud beneath the German tank and the British artillery shells continued bursting all around him. The sky was ablaze with the light of the explosions. The ground shook with their force, and then rose into the air in pieces, like a geyser, only to cascade downwards again, rattling all over the metal of the tank. He covered his head and ears and groaned. He had enough of this bloody war! By God, he had! At twenty-two years of age, he felt <u>old</u>. Damn old, and tired; so tired that the very bones of his body felt malleable, even watery. He no longer cared who won, or how. He no longer thought in terms of 'them and us'. The whole thing had become a personal struggle, a supreme effort, physical and mental, for his own survival. He had cared once, but that was a very time long time.

He had been in the Wehrmacht for only two years, but in this comparatively short period of time, he had been to Denmark for basic training, which had been intensely hard and very basic. It had been cruel and bitter fighting on the white hell of the Russian front, where he had been painfully, but not seriously wounded in the right elbow. The Russian experience had destroyed totally whatever illusions he held about 'glory' and 'fighting for the Vaderland.' These illusions were rapidly disappeared in the whirling snow, and he shivered again now as he remembered the penetrating cold, so cold that the very air was almost a tangible thing, and they had desperately struggled to cover all their exposed skin with their inadequate clothing to prevent the frostbite they all dreaded. To be wounded had been, in a way, almost a relief, for this had meant that he was sent back to the Russian front, and he spent some time in a French convent which had been commanded for use as a German military hospital. This had not too bad, but as soon as he regained the use of his right arm, he was sent out again, and here he was, right in the thick of it all. He just wanted the way out…anywhere!

He was tall and slimly built. Good looking in the established Teutonic tradition, with brown hair brushed smoothly back along the side of his head, cut short at the back, and a small moustache. He had lived a perfectly ordinary comfortable life with his parents, and his brother, Fritz, in the town of Hamburg, where both he and Fritz had played together in a small amateur jazz band. They had some high old times that they enjoyed. He had a good job in a local engineering works, which had suited him well, for he had always been good with his hands, and a genuine love for machinery. Never for one moment had he ever had any doubts about the war. He had never been a man of strong political persuasion, never had been much of a one for attending meetings and agitating, but rather tended to attempt to enjoy his life as much as possible. He had many friends; there had been parties, girlfriends, outings into the surrounding countryside, visits to the local beer cellar where they had all sat until the early hours of the morning, talking. As many visits to the theatre as he could afford. He had a reasonably paid job, and carefully apportioned his wage, putting aside just a little for savings. He liked clothes, and he liked 'good' clothes.

His mother said he was something of a 'dandy' but he enjoyed the feeling of being well-dressed, and was rather proud of his wardrobe where everything was clean and well-pressed.

He was, like most Germans, law-abiding by nature, and liked order, tidiness and discipline. He thought Hitler was a great man, and when Germany entered the war, he had been ready and willing to fight for the Führer and the

4

Third Reich. He had no doubts about it all. It was up to Germany to save the world. Germany was right, it was quite obvious to Herbert, and all the Führer wanted was to make things better for everybody. He said so, and Herbert and Fritz believed him. He had saved Germany before, in the terrible days of the Thirties, and he would do it again. Herbert never doubted for a moment. But that was before…

Now it was autumn 1944, on a lousy grey, wet morning, and here he was, stuck under an abandoned German tank, pinned down on his belly with his face pressed into the mud of French soil, waiting for his mate, Helmut.

For the last four days, the whole German front had been in retreat, including Herbert's Regiment. Everybody was moving, continuously, but where to exactly only God knew, for no one else seemed to. No one could find out what was happening, all they knew was that seemed to be surrounded by shells. They marched, and were joined by 'strays' who marched behind them. 'For all the world like some bloody Pied Piper', thought Herbert. They ran, and suddenly everybody was running. They moved forwards, then backwards, sometimes Herbert reckoned from looking at the sky that they must have marched in almost a complete circle. They did not take their clothes off for weeks, and inside their boots, their feet were swollen and rubbed raw and bloody, but they dared not to remove the boots, for they would never have been able to put them on again. Brief rest periods only seemed to make them more exhausted, then on again, their legs moving like those of an automaton, and their eyes staring unseeingly to the front, like those of the 'undead' in the old horror films that Herbert used to enjoy at the local cinema so very long ago.

He never quite understood how it happened, but Herbert found himself stranded in a French village about thirty kilometres from Caen, with three others and a wireless truck. He had his orders. He was supposed to wait for the retreat of the last infantry line of the Wehrmacht which, he was told, would take place at about ten o'clock that night. When they had all gone, he was to retrieve the telephone cable that linked to the last of the infantry with the artillery, and then he was to follow them. The regimental staff had already gone. 'Which doesn't surprise me', he thought, 'it's a bit too active here for them'.

It was getting near midnight, and there was no sign of the last of the infantry, so Herbert and Helmut decided that they would venture out and see if they could find any sign of activity at all.

They left the other two with the truck, and set off warily. A farm building loomed out of the darkness, and they made their way towards it, approaching quietly and with excess caution. At first, they could hear nothing, and dropping flat on their bellies, they began to crawl as silently as possible over the tussock ground. Suddenly they heard sounds, and saw vague shadowy movements.

"It's them, ok" Helmut said in a low voice. "What the hell are they messing at here?" And he started to get on his feet.

"Get down," Herbert said, listening intently. "They're talking about bloody fun then," and easing forward, he peered gingerly around the side of the barn. "Their tin hats are different! Mein Gott! They're not ours, they're Tommies!" And he flung himself flat on his face.

There were mere yards between them. Thank God it was a dark night. Herbert's heart beat like a sledge hammer in his chest until he felt sure that the Tommies must hear it from where they stood, in a group, just a short distance from him. He turned cautiously and looked at Helmut.

He dared not speak, even in a whisper, and in fact, he doubted if he could have done so, but he raised his eyebrows and Helmut understood. He gently raised his right arm and made scissors signs with the first two fingers of his right arm. Herbert nodded, and easing on to his side, he extracted a small pair of pliers from his pocket. His fingers explored, and at length found the telephone cable.

It was cut through in a minute, and the link between the infantry and the artillery was served, according to instructions.

The only thing left to do was to get the hell out of there as quickly as possible. Still lying flat, they edged backwards, and not until the barn was completely out of sight, did they rise to their feet and run, in a crouching position, keeping beneath their hedge and taking advantage of all shelter, back towards the deserted village. The truck was still there where they had left it, but there was no sign of life around it at all. The other two had disappeared and only the abandoned houses and farms stood with sightless eyes. The expected last of the infantry had not appeared, and the truth eventually dawned upon Herbert and Helmut. There was no bloody infantry. They were not coming, they had not got through, they had all been either captured or killed. Herbert and Helmut were all that was left, and here they were, stuck, all on their own, in a little pocket in an alien landscape, and completely surrounded by the enemy. Now what?

They had absolutely no idea which direction they should take, and no true idea of what was happening around them, or what had happened to their infantry. Helmut kept on muttering to himself, "The bastards! The bastards! The bloody bastards!" but it was not very clear to Herbert just who he meant.

They could think of nothing else to do, so they clambered into the truck, and drove off in the general direction of where they thought the German lines should be. The shell fire was continuous, and Herbert, driving, swerved violently and zigzagged from side to side in hope this might prevent a direct hit on the truck. Helmut was being thrown all around, and continued to curse, mindlessly, and fluently, repeating each phrase over and over again. At length, they ran into a veritable barrage directly in front of them, and Herbert braked hard. The doors flew open, and both half fell, half jumped out. "Well that's that then," Herbert said with an air of finality.

"We've had it. There's hardly any petrol left in the bloody thing anyway we couldn't go much further."

Helmut stared at him. "What the hell are we going to do then?

"I don't know! Keep going I suppose. But they're not having this bleeding truck."

Suddenly it seemed very important to Herbert that the truck should not fall into enemy hands. Why, he didn't know. It could hardly have made a difference anyway, but at that moment, he was filled with only one thought. The enemy must not have the truck.

He found a grenade, and shouted Helmut to run. Pulling the pin, he lobbed the grenade into the back of the vehicle, and then, hands over his head and crouching, he ran like hell himself. The grenade exploded, and the truck flew up into the air into small pieces.

They began to walk, to run, to crawl, taking as much advantage of any cover offered by the terrain as they could. The whole night was filled with the sound of fury, but they caught a glimpse of another human being. They still entertained the faint hope that they might get catch up with their mates, might still run into some organised Germans that might not be lost.

Another farmhouse was thrown into the silhouette, lit from behind by bursting shells and the first threads of morning in the sky.

'A bit of shelter at least', thought Herbert, and grabbing hold of Helmut by the arm, pointed him towards it. They made their way cautiously towards where they supposed the back door might have been. It opened into what had once been a large and pleasant room, with a big open fireplace along one side. Some family pictures still hung drunkenly on the walls, and the tattered remnants of lowers curtains clung limply to the broken window panes. Herbert noticed, with the detached interest, that some pot dogs were still intact on the high mantelpiece, and between them stood a green glazed vase with some late roses in it, now mud on the floor. He thought fleetingly of the people who had lived here, of the lady of the house cutting the roses and putting them in the vase. This had once been someone's home.

The room was full of German soldiers. They were leaning in the corners, sitting on the floor, or one or two chairs left behind when the occupants had fled. They were not moving much, just waiting quietly. They took no notice of Herbert and Helmut as they burst in. What were two amongst so many?

Like Herbert and Helmut, they had had enough. They were bewildered, confused and they had stopped. Stopped feeling, stopped fighting, stopped firing, stopped running, stopped moving, stopped thinking. Now they wanted the shelling to stop, and the killing to stop, and leave them alone. They thought capture inevitable, and they waited for it to engulf them.

They stared unblinkingly in front of them. A couple glanced towards the newcomers, but no one spoke. Some were smoking, drawing on the cigarette desperately and letting the smoke slide slowly down their nostrils before passing the cigarette to the soldier standing next to them. They were all haggard eyes, mud-spattered and unkempt. Those by the fireplace shuffled up a little so that Herbert and Helmut could sit on the floor, and where they had settled and the sound of movement ceased. Again, there was silence.

Suddenly, there in the corner, was a young German officer of the S.S. not long out of the military school: still wet behind the ears in Herbert's judgement, the bloom of excessive youth still on his side with extravagant sweeps of his arm. "They were all dogs," he said, "to give up so easily."

They were all yellow and had no courage. They were a disgrace. He was going to have them lined up against a wall and shot for treason as soon as he could. They were traitors, and had forgotten the honour due to their beloved Führer… The glory of the Vaderland. The honour and the might of Germany… They were cowards… The honour of the German army… His voice rose higher, and tears streamed down his face. He became incoherent and began to sob. No one answered him. No one spoke. There was nothing to say, and they all had heard it all before. No one seemed to hear until a middle-aged, worn out infantryman slumped on the floor near to the young man, rose slowly and painfully to his feet. His hands sought and found the rifle he had thrown down, and with what seemed the last of his failing strength, he raised it above his head, and brought the butt down on the young officer's head. He fell heavily to the floor, and once again there was silence. Two of the other rose to their feet, and threw the young man out of the door.

"What the hell does he know about anything?" one of them muttered. Herbert heard the young man's body hit the ground outside.

The fireplace was immense, and made of stone, and Herbert, looking upwards, could see the small square at the top of the chimney brightly illuminated with bursting shells.

'God! It only wants just one of them to come down that, and a right mess we shall be in'. The thought flashed across his mind, and the deed immediately followed. There was a blinding flash, splinters, shrapnel, flying wood and stone everywhere. Most of the men were buried beneath the rubble, and some of them screamed as plaster filled their lungs. Those able to move were struggling wildly to where the door had been, panic-stricken. Helmut made it out, and looked around for Herbert, but could not find him. Turning around, he fought his way back into the shell of the farmhouse, and found Herbert trapped by a fallen beam. For a minute he thought he was dead, and crouching down, put his head on Herbert's chest to see if he could find a heartbeat. He was still alive, but unconscious. Helmut began tearing away at the wood and rubble, breaking his nails and shredding the skin on his hands, and again muttering, "The bastards! The bastards!" half choking on the smoke and dust. He worked desperately, and grabbing Herbert beneath the arms he dragged him clear. He only just made it outside when the rest of the building collapsed totally, burying totally those remaining inside.

Helmut dragged Herbert well away from the smoking pile of wood and stone that had once been a farmhouse, and propped him against a hedge. He slapped him on the face, still muttering, and in sudden moment of panic, grabbed him by the shoulders and shook him, his head lolled backwards and forwards.

"Water," he muttered, "find some water!" He was wildly looking around. Shells were still bursting, and the air was full of flying clods of earth, fragments of earth, and small stones. He found what had once been a water trough for animals, and at the bottom was a shallow depth of brackish water. He scooped it up in his cupped arms, and crouching, ran back and dashed it into Herbert's still face.

He repeated this several times, half whispering, half sobbing, "For Christ's sake! Oh God! For Christ's sake!" over and over again.

Herbert only actually remained unconscious for some fifteen minutes, but to Helmut it seemed like hours. At length, he opened his eyes and tried to sit up straight. This seemed to be an enormous effort, his head pounded, his vision blurred. He began to cough, and then vomited. Helmut remembered that neither of them had eaten for the last twenty-four hours.

Herbert was found to be bleeding badly from a deep gash in his right thigh, and as he looked at it, he could see the whiteness of the bone. Try as they would, they could not hold the edges of the cut together, and the blood continued welling up and pumping out. Helmut dug into the back of his mind, and remembered a little first aid kit. He dragged Herbert out of his tunic, and grabbed hold of the sleeve of his shirt, tearing it off at the shoulder. He searched for a piece of stick, and wrapping the sleeve around Herbert's thigh, and using the stick as a 'key' he fashioned a tourniquet, holding it until the bleeding eventually stopped. Herbert struggled to his feet, but he could barely stand.

"We've got to get the hell out of here," Helmut muttered, and dragging Herbert's arm over his shoulder, he staggered off, half supporting him, pausing every few minutes to let Herbert rest. They made very slow progress, and the thigh wound opened again, and Herbert felt the blood running into his boots.

Eventually, they spotted a German tank with a white flag still flying from the tower.

"Let's head for that," Helmut said. "If we get underneath it, at least we have some shelter from these bloody everlasting shells." He looked at Herbert, and thought he was about to pass out again. He was obviously in great pain, but they had to find some shelter. They were just sitting ducks out there in the open. Helmut grabbed him by the shoulders again, and eventually got him to the tank. He shoved him under as far as he could, and pulled some undergrowth over his legs in a faint attempt at camouflage.

"Lie still, for Christ's sake. Don't try to move," he said. "I'll go and see if I can find a field dressing station or something. There must be some medical aid somewhere. Then I'll come back for you. Lie here and shut up!" Herbert was only too thankful to be told to lie still. It was unnecessary because in any case, for the moment, he was incapable of movement. His whole world was filled with pain. His leg throbbed incessantly, his head was filled with cotton wool, his world vision was still blurred, and every fibre in his being ached.

'God,' he thought, 'I wished I could pass out again. I wish I could stay unconscious until the bloody lot is over. Then I wish those silly fools would understand that this bleeding tank had been abandoned....'

He pushed his face into the soft earth, and its sharp smell caught in his nostrils. He lay quite still, on the edge of unconsciousness, and occasionally drifting over it. Time ceased to have any meaning. He knew it was daylight, he still heard the continuous shelling, but the noise seemed to come forward and flow back, like waves on the shore, and his thoughts became a bewildering mixture of present horror and childhood recollections.

In fact, it did not take Helmut very long to locate a field dressing station, and when he returned to the abandoned tank, Herbert seemed to be fully conscious again. Dragging him out was intensely painful, and the bleeding began afresh, so he could not walk at all. Helmut stooping down, got him on to his back, with his arms over Helmut's shoulders, and his legs hanging loosely, and with a super human effort, he staggered in the direction of the dressing station.

With intense relief, Helmut handed Herbert over to the ministrations of medical staff and left him there. Herbert did not see him again.

The chaos inside the dressing station was as bad as outside, for wounded were being brought in from all directions, some being dragged by their comrades, who were themselves on the verge of total exhaustion, some crawled unaided, and others borne on stretchers. When Herbert's turn came, he was bandaged up and made as comfortable as possible, and had a ticket pinned on his tunic with his name, rank, number and regiment. Then he was told to wait in a nearby barn, and he hobbled over to it with some difficulty, but he was beginning to feel a bit better. The firm bandage supported his leg, the bleeding had stopped, and although his head still ached abominably, he regained his sense, and knew what was going on around him.

When he entered the barn, the sight that met his eyes was to remain with him in nightmares for weeks to come. The floor was covered with straw, and soldiers lay upon it, row by row. All of them wounded, and some shot to pieces, beyond hope. One man in the corner did not seem to have much of his face left, one youngster was screaming with his belly ripped open, there were pads of blood-soaked bandages where limbs had once been, there were men with appalling burns, who had been trapped in a blazing tank, and dragged out with their clothes ablaze. The air was filled with the harsh sound of pain. There was a smell of blood, and unwashed clothing, and of stale vomit.

Herbert found himself a corner to sit down in, and he tried to make his leg more comfortable by rolling his tunic, and using it as a pad upon which to rest it. He found his cheeks were wet with tears. On one side of him was one young S.S. officer ('Oh! Not again,' he thought), whose leg had been blown off below the knee, and who seemed to be mercifully unconscious, and on the other side of him a chap from the Luftwaffe, whose plane had been shot down, and burst into flames. He had managed by some miracle to get out alive, but both of his hands were charred lumps of flesh, and Herbert could see the whiteness of the bone as he held them out in front of him.

The shelling had intensified and was getting nearer. Stray bullets penetrated the wall of the barn in one corner and two of the wounded were put beyond more agony. Splinters of burst shell showered through the roof! The whole place looked like a charnel house.

For a fleeting moment, Herbert remembered one of the very early air raids on Hamburg. He had been on night shift, and was cycling home in the early hours of the morning when he had seen a cattle wagon that had been carrying beasts to the railway station and a waiting goods train. It never made it, and Herbert could see the wrecked wagon, the smouldering straw, and the scattered, ripped, dismembered carcasses flung about the street.

He looked around him, in this barn, and for the first time, he thought 'This is it! This is the end. I'll never come out of this lot alive!' He crouched down, and covered his head in a vain attempt to shut out the noise of the unceasing shelling, and the sights of the inside of the barn.

Hours seemed to pass, and at length one of the medical officers appeared.

"We are running out of medical supplies," he said, "and we can do no more for the wounded here. We are going to try and get you all out. That is, if we can, and the best way we can. We are sending for a doctor with a small patrol over to the enemy lines, to see if we can negotiate."

Almost as he spoke an ambulance with a red cross flag on the left-hand side, and a white flag on the right, drove off in the direction of the shelling, and very soon afterwards the gunfire stopped. They could not believe it! At first, the silence, broken only by the low groans of the wounded, seemed uncanny, and almost hurt their ears. Then the word came. "The enemy will give us twenty minutes and will hold their fire for that time, to give us a chance to get the wounded out. Those who can walk will do so. The rest will be driven, since some transport is available. There is no time to lose, we only have twenty minutes. Hurry up!"

Herbert, the eternal optimist, felt a new surge of hope. His luck had not deserted him; it looked as though he was going to get out of this lot after all. He struggled to his feet, and found that the rest had improved his leg considerably. He could even walk. Not very well, but he could walk, and leave the limited transport free for those who could not. He was right out of the barn and halfway across the yard, before he could remember his tunic. He retraced his steps, but found that he could not go back in. The doorway was full of people helping each other, off stretchers, and medics attempting to hurry everybody along, and reminding them that they only had twenty minutes. He thought 'the hell with the bloody tunic' and then caught sight of a pile of clothing assorted in shapes and sizes, probably removed from the dead. He picked up the top tunic in the pile and put that on.

Outside there were British soldiers everywhere, and they kept on shouting 'Mag Schnell.' It was the first time that Herbert actually come face-to-face with 'the enemy' and he was somehow faintly surprised. The place was alive with ambulances, trucks, cars. Lack of sleep, pain, hunger, and the crack on the head all combined to cloud Herbert's brain, and he could not fully understand what was happening. The medical officer has said that they were going to try and get them all out, hadn't he? Well, why hadn't they? And what were the British doing here, running around herding them up like so many sheep, and shouting orders in very bad German? They seemed to expect everybody to understand them, and Herbert couldn't. It was chaos all over again. Herbert gave up trying to make sense out of the whole bloody business, and just followed everybody else to wherever they were going.

After about twenty minutes, they left the farm, and the barn, passed through the scattered and deserted ruins of the village, and turned down a lane with a high hedgerow on either side. In front of him, Herbert saw the gateway into a field, and just inside it were six tanks. The ragged straggling column drew to a halt.

A British soldier looked out of the first tank, and shouted derisively "Heil Hitler! Deutschland Kaputt!" and gave a mock Nazi salute. Herbert looked at him, and the six British tanks, and realisation dawned. The British had taken over. They had not been 'got out' as the medical officer had said, but taken prisoner in the hands of the enemy!

Somehow, in his confused state of mind, he had fondly imagined that by some miracle they would all have been sent back to German lines... Eventually meet up with those units still fighting. Exactly how, he did not know. He had no means of knowing where the fighting line was, or indeed if it still existed at all. But it never occurred to him that he would find himself a prisoner of war.

He looked down at himself. His clothing was in rags, his trouser legs stiff with dried blood, his face and hands bruised, scratched and he was filthy. He was smeared with dried mud, he was exhausted and hungry. He then discovered that the tunic he had so carelessly picked up belonged to an S.S. officer, and he looked about him wildly. He had heard something about what the British thought of the S.S. and felt he could expect little from them if they thought he was a member of this hated group. But it was the only covering he had, and it was cold. He could not discard it now! He decided to keep it on, and risk it.

There seemed to be about sixty of the wounded in all, left alive that is, and they were quickly over by the British Medical Corps. The very seriously wounded here were quickly driven away to the nearest hospital. Dressings were changed, and everybody was patched up as well as possible with the limited facilities available. Then they were on the march again, but only twenty of them now, and in the charge of the six guards.

Not that this was really necessary, for they were all in very bad shape, and lacked the strength to make a run for it. And where to anyway?

After about an hour, they came to an orchard. Very fresh and green it looked, with the ripening fruit for the most part on the trees. A make-shift camp had been set up in here, and some three hundred or so Germans were already in it. Herbert noted that same pattern as before. They all just simply stopped. They were haggard and unkempt, their faces and the tattered remnants of their uniforms filthy, and their bodies slumped with total physical and mental fatigue.

Barbed wire had been put in roughly all around, and in each corner, conveniently stationed in an apple tree, sat a British soldier with a Bren gun. Everybody was ordered to sit down, and thankfully they obeyed.

It was a temporarily quiet, and Herbert let his thoughts flow. 'That's that then! That's the end of the bloody lot!' He accepted this with a stoicism of the fatalist. There was nothing else, and there was not going to be. No more fighting for the Vaderland, for the Führer. No more fighting for anybody.

The once-proud German army seemed to have been reduced to a mere handful of ragged, gaunt men sitting around him on the grass. And there was no more fight left in any of them, by the look of it.

For Herbert the war was over, and the strange new existence was about to begin. He was in a kind of limbo, a vacuum between the old life and whatever the future held. He was behind the barbed wire… He was that hitherto unknown quantity. He was a prisoner of war.

Chapter II:

Transit Camp in France

That night in the orchard was a long one, probably the longest Herbert had ever known. Shortly after midnight, it began to rain, not heavily, but with relentless persistence. The German prisoners remained sitting on the wet ground, and tried surreptitiously to move closer together for warmth. Coat collars were turned up around numbed ears, and hands plunged into the thin pockets of tunics. The order has been to sit down, and in attempt to do this, Herbert soon found the muscles in the back of his legs tightening to cramp. Then, with nothing to lean back on, a nagging ache began at the base of his spine.

By dawn, most of the prisoners were shuffling restlessly, and the Tommies, armed and sitting in the trees like so many birds of prey, were wary and suspicious of every movement. A short burst of Bren gun fire into the air brought temporary stillness. A field canteen arrived and everyone was issued with a mug of tea and six biscuits. The tea, if not very good, was at least hot, and the prisoners cupped their cold hands around the tin mugs gratefully. It had been a long time since they had eaten or had anything warm inside them.

Herbert had almost forgotten his wound. The dressings that had been applied were both comforting and soothing, and in any case, it no longer seemed very important. All he could think about was what was going to happen to him, and to all of them. He had no idea of how the British treated prisoners of war, and he could make no attempt at guessing where they would be taken. How much longer were they to be kept sitting on wet grass in this orchard? Herbert was exceedingly uncomfortable. The hot tea had gone straight through him, and the call of nature had become very pressing. He looked around, and it seemed that it was this effect on most of them. No one dared to get up and go behind a tree, with the British, fingers on triggers, watching every move. They shuffled about miserably, and then someone got up. They had to! This startled the guards into activity, and guns were immediately trained upon the prisoner, who raised both of his hands above his head in the traditional gesture, and walked slowly across to a convenient tree. The guards realised what was happening, and tension eased slightly. Within the next few minutes every tree in the apple orchard was well watered!

Army trucks arrived, and the prisoners were ordered, through an interpreter, to stand in file in ranks of three. They counted for the first time, and soldiers and prisoners in close proximity, looked at each other curiously. Until now, the war had been something of a distance long affair to most of them, and now they were virtually face-to-face for the first time. Each side found that the other looked just as ordinary as themselves. The Germans looked old, tired and hungry. The British, on average, younger, in better shape, and bloody fed up!

After the preliminaries, everyone was loaded on the trucks, under guard, and the mystery journey started. Two hours or more passed according to Herbert's reckoning, with the truck driver swerving and skidding over rough and bumpy ground. No one had any idea of where they were going, or in which direction they were headed, and in any case, they didn't care anymore. Eventually, the truck stopped.

"Alles Raus! Raus! Mag Schnell!" came the order. "Come on! Come on! Get a bloody move on! Schnell!" The Tommy seemed to like this bit of German, probably the only phrase of any language many of them had. They repeated it often enough, and Herbert thought it sounded like damned odd on the lips of the 'enemy.' Once again, file, ranks of three, and count. Surely, they can't think anyone could have slipped off? No one had the strength of get far, and in any case, the only place was to go back into the shellfire.

In front of them was a huge compound, full of tents, and totally surrounded by barbed wire. By the look of it, it was already full or prisoners. This aspect was a daunting image, but at least with a bit of luck, they would be under cover, which seemed one degree better than the apple orchard of the previous night.

Before they were allowed to enter, everyone was searched, very thoroughly. Herbert didn't know what they could be looking for, unless it was hidden weapons. All personal belongings were peremptorily confiscated. Rings, wrist watches, pocket knives, letters, private papers, photographs, pay books, money. In fact, everything. Then it was Herbert's turn. The Tommy looked at him, and gave a twisted grin. His eyes were hard, and his attitude entirely without compassion, but Herbert did not expect that anyway, for at the moment, he was defeated! And the Tommy was the 'victor.' His belongings looked like a pitiful little pile, and the Tommy turned everything over with a podgy hand. Herbert only carried one photograph with him, a snapshot which he had himself taken of his mother in the garden of the house in Hamburg, in much happier days. She was standing on the neat piece of land at the back of the house, self-conscious, slightly smiling. The Tommy picked it up and looked hard at it. Then maliciously he tore it across, and across again into four pieces. He handed the pieces to Herbert. "Alles Kaputt," he said, and laughed. Herbert felt anger rise within him, but he said nothing.

Once inside the compound some kind of order seemed to be established, and German officers had been put in charge of the prisoners. Herbert was assigned to Tent No.27, with twenty-four others, and Walter Ziegler, a Feldwebel (sergeant) was to be their leader. It was his job to keep peace and order, and to make sure that everybody was alright. He seemed like a decent, earnest book-ish sort of chap, and undoubtedly he took his duties very seriously.

The prisoners were, as may be expected, a truly assorted bunch. They came from the infantry, the artillery, Panzer Corps, Luftwaffe, the S.S. and two from a marine commando. They were each supplied with two blankets, a spoon and a fork, a Billy can and a tin mug. As Herbert made up his bed on the ground, he found himself next to a member of the Panzer Corps, who introduced himself as Gerhard Winkler.

"What happened to you lot?" Winkler asked him.

"Got bleeding-well caught, right in the middle," Herbert said.

"God, what a mess! And then, as if that wasn't enough, I got wounded, for the second bloody time. My leg this time! I never thought I'd get out alive, and I wouldn't have done if it hadn't been for my mate, Helmut. God knows how he did it, but he dragged me out, and saved my life! I should have been killed, but for him. I don't know what happened to him after… I hope he's alright, somewhere!"

"Alles Raus!" The order echoed around the Camp.

'Christ!' Herbert thought, only half-awake. 'Bleeding orders again!' It seemed to him as though his entire life of the latter years had been nothing but bloody orders. All around him, prisoners were crawling out of their blankets, and pulling on their bits of clothing discarded the night before. The word went around that there was some food on the way. Further orders were issued, and a long queue formed in a single file outside the canteen tent. They were all incredibly hungry, and jostled each other in their anxiety to get nearer the food.

Every prisoner was issued with a Billy can of water, six biscuits, and a quarter portion of bully beef. That was it! Herbert walked slowly, still limping slightly, back to the tent, and sat down and looked at his food. He was bloody hungry! Light-headed with hunger. So was everyone else, and as he looked around, he saw that most of them had eaten most of their rations before they got back to their tents. They were walking back from the direction of the canteen, with their mouths crammed full, and tipping back the Billy cans of water.

Herbert began to eat, forcing himself to take it slowly, and chewing every mouthful, not only in an effort to make it last a bit longer, but he felt that he was not careful, his stomach would revolt against the lumpy, cold food after so long, and he would vomit. He needed the strength the food gave him, and he knew he needed it badly. Dry sweet stale biscuits and bully beef did not really go together very well, but he was grateful for it. He was about to bite into his last biscuit, when Feldwebel Ziegler returned to the tent rather agitated.

"Listen! Listen you lot," he said. "The rations you have just been given are to last twenty-four hours. Supplies are short, and because the English are taking more German prisoners every day, they just can't cope! There is just not enough food to go around! So, you had better take it easy!"

The prisoners began to murmur.

"I know! I know," he said apologetically. "We are all bloody hungry, but there's damn all we can do about it. The food just isn't there, and we are in the hands of the enemy. The camp commandant hopes to improve the situation soon, but for the moment… take it easy! Ration it out… especially the drinking water!"

Poor old Ziegler! He was doing his utmost to be fair. His face shone with earnestness, and his eyes were worried. Herbert looked ruefully at his last biscuit. Then he looked at the sun, and as far as he could tell, it was about mid-morning, but there was no way of knowing the exact time, because none of them had a watch left. Or they shouldn't have!

'Twenty-four hours', he thought. So what should he do? Eat the last biscuit now, and suffer further hunger pangs later on? Or save it? The water too. Would it be better to quench his thirst now, drink it all in one go, or hoard it and use it to wet his lips every hour? He ate the last biscuit! Tomorrow, he decided, he would divide his rations up properly. He would divide his share up properly, get organised, apportion things out... tomorrow.

The other prisoners in the tent continued to grumble, and the muttering went on, but in the end, they had to accept it. They were prisoners of war, in the hands of the enemy, and there was nothing else they could do.

When they had eaten, one of two of the prisoners chatting desultorily, strolled around the compound, hoping perhaps to see a familiar face from their own unit. There were hundreds of them in this camp. Young ones, obviously, middle-aged, understandably. But some old. They looked so old and frail that they should have never been called up and forced into this fighting. They were too old to stand the pace, to take the hardship. They all looked dishevelled and hollow-eyed, but so far at least, they seemed to be standing up alright. Herbert supposed vaguely that if the British were going to dispose of prisoners, they would have done something about it before now, so presumably they were going to treat then in accordance with the Geneva Convention.

As they loitered in the compound, their hands in their pockets. Herbert searched among the passing faces hoping that perhaps Helmut might be here. But he did not see him. He felt sure that he must have been taken prisoner, for he could not have got out! No one could have got out of that mess. Perhaps he had been sent to some other camp. They had been through a lot together, he and Helmut, and had got to know each other fairly well. He supposed the old-fashioned phrase 'comrade in arms' would be the right one to use. He certainly owed Helmut a debt that he would not be able to forget in a hurry, and his thoughts dwelt again on that room in the farmhouse, the haggard hopeless faces, the splintering shell, the rubble and the weight across his hips, pinning him fast. He felt again real fear!

At length, he did spot one face he knew. Horst Botteler, who had been the regimental dispatch rider. Good old Horst! The ace of two wheels... Thank God for that at least!

"Horst," he shouted. "Horst Botteler!" and then he ran towards him, with a lop-sized stiff legged gait. "How the hell did you get here? Are there any others from our lot?"

From Horst he learned what happened. The whole of the regiment, staff, the rest of the telephone and Morse unit had received a direct hit from the enemy shelling. They were all killed outright. There were no survivors. None. No one had escaped. The news numbed him. "Are you sure?" he half whispered. Horst was sure! They were both quiet for a minute, remembering some of the others of their unit. They had been a good bunch, and even in the last few days, it had been share and share alike. There had been a good spirit among them, and now they were all dead. All of them, dead! And for what? What the hell was good of it all? Was there any purpose behind this wholesale slaughter that he could not see? What a God-awful waste it all was.

Herbert remembered young Hans, the 'baby' of the unit. A youth still in his teens, honest, bewildered and still so inexperienced and naïve that it hurt. They all had tried to look after him a bit; for them, he had been the younger brother of them all.

"Hans?" he asked Horst.

Horst nodded. "Hans too!" he said. "All of them. Everybody!"

His shoulders slumped.

For a moment Herbert felt something akin to despair. He was not an introspective man. He was a fatalist, and basically, he accepted, almost without any question, what fate and the Gods saw fit to bestow upon him. If he could turn it to his advantage, then he did so. If not, he would just bear it until it changed. But this was a bitter pill to have to swallow. They were all dead, and he, Herbert, was still alive, and he could not help but be glad that he was.

If he hadn't been ordered to remain behind with the truck in that shattered, shelled, deserted French village that he couldn't even remember the name of, he would have been with the others. He would have been dead too! And in spite of everything, in spite of his present situation, and in spite of sincerely mourning their loss, he was still glad to be alive.

After last roll-call, the camp settled down for the night. Still hungry, most prisoners were wakeful. They did not sleep very easily, but took what rest they could in a series of naps. It was a bright clear night, crisp and starlit, and the battle still raging. Enemy bombers droned overhead, filling the air of waves of sound, heading towards Germany, and Herbert thought of his home in Hamburg.

In the last letter he had received from his mother, she briefly mentioned bombing. One or two familiar buildings were no longer standing. She was alone now, for his father was called upon at the age of fifty-nine. How on earth would he manage, Herbert worried. He had never been very strong, and the marching alone could finish him off. His brother, Fritz, was a weapon-master in the 5th Paratroop Regiment, and at least when his mother wrote the letter, he was still safe and well. Would 'they' let his mother know that he was a prisoner of war? She might think he had been killed. Surely they would send some official notification so that she would know that he was alright? They did that, didn't they? They had his number, his name and regiment. They had been most insistent upon this. They asked his 'next of kin'. Surely they would send something? He could not. If she heard any news about the fighting, she would know he must have been right in the thick of it, and she would be very fearful. At length, troubled in mind, and aching with hunger, he fell into a fitful sleep.

They spent about three weeks in this camp. The daily ration did not change, but Herbert eventually got it worked out to a fine art. He would eat five biscuits every day, and save one. This would mean that by Sunday, he would have seven extra biscuits, and he could look forward to it, and have a real feast.

Ever since he was a child, they always had something extra special, extra nice to eat on Sundays at home, and therefore, even to adult Herbert, Sunday was the day to have a feast. Suddenly, the whole thing seemed so trivial. That hunger should drive grown men to the counting of biscuit crumbs. He had little thought that he would ever see the day when saving of a dry biscuit, and ways to make it last, would occupy most of his waking thoughts. A dry biscuit that in normal circumstances, he would not have eaten at all, for he did not really like biscuits, and had thrown better than this out to the birds, before the war. Ah! Before the war! That was the difference. That was a long time ago, centuries... aeons ago.

By Wednesday, he had three extra biscuits carefully saved. He looked at them avidly. He put them in a safe place, then furtively retrieved them and looked at them again. He ate one, and put the other two away. Then he went through the whole damned pantomime again. He ate all three! And all the time, the little man inside his head was saying 'Herbert! Herbert! All this fuss over a little dry biscuit?' and apologetically, he answered 'I know! I know!'

This next day, Thursday, he had start saving all over again. This happened all the time, and try as he would to stiffen his will power, never ever did he get to save the whole seven, and have the 'feast' he planned. The hunger pangs in his belly always won over the little man inside his head!

Gerhard Schreibar, an ex-S.S. paratrooper, was a chain smoker. Or rather he had been. Now he had not been able to have a cigarette for days, and he was suffering. He felt as if he was slowly going around the bend. He was desperate for a drag, and this desperate need was aggravated by the same hunger that was gnawing at everybody's guts. It got so bad that he could not keep still.

He developed jerks and twitches, and his hands shook horribly. For the first time in his life he began to bite his fingers, and indeed bit them so far down that the quicks bled. So far, the thought ruefully, that was the 'war round' he had received! He knew he must have a smoke if he was going to survive.

Somehow, by dexterous sleight of hand, he had managed to retain his wrist watch, even though he too had been searched at the gates of the compound like everybody else, and quite suddenly, he had an idea. He thought it was over, there was no doubt that it was damn risky, but he was determined to try it, because this time, he would have walked through a hall of bullets for a cigarette.

He had been watching the British guards patrolling the barbed wire perimeter of the camp, and he noticed there was one, a smallish chap, who looked – at least to Gerhard – just a bit simple, a bit gullible, in face a soft touch. Gerhard had always been a bit of a 'trader,' and in that long ago before the war, had pulled off quite a few profitable deals, none of which seemed half as important as this one. He was sure that if he could only embark upon a bit of conversation with this guard, he could fix up something. This issue was, how to get talking. Gerhard had a few phrases of schoolroom English, but althoughhe could speak only a little, he understood a great deal more.

He mustered up his courage, and choosing a time when the right guard was on duty, he strolled in the direction of wire. He stood, hands in his pockets, scuffing the dust with the toe of his boot, and from beneath his lowered eyes, he watched the Tommy aimlessly walking up and down outside the wire, pursuing some pattern of patrol known only to himself. As the man once again turned his direction, Gerhard straightened up, and pointing, he shouted at the guard, "You enjoy zis bloody war?"

The guard was startled and suspicious. You could never tell with these damn Jerries. He knew that. He read all of the papers, and knew about these Germans. Didn't they keep on saying, over in England, that the only good Jerry was a dead one? He was taking no chances, not him! "You get back from that wire," he ordered Gerhard, and pointed his rifle straight at his head.

28

Gerhard raised his hands.

"Alright! Ok!" he said. "I just try to make talk!"

"We're not allowed to talk to you, so move on or I'll bloody well make fire, and make sure you don't talk!"

Gerhard turned slowly away, and then quickly he whipped around, and shouted to the guard, "What time is it?"

"I don't know! Haven't got a watch," the man replied.

This was Gerhard's chance. It was now or never. He surreptitiously drew his watch out of his pocket, and dangled it in front of the guard from about three feet away, and held it at arm's length.

"Good," he said. "Swiss made! Nothing but good for the S.S.!"

The Tommy was puzzled, but definitely interested and tempted, Gerhard could see that, and he watched the man's eyes flickering around to make sure that they were not observed.

"How much?" he said.

"Two hundred cigarettes," Gerhard replied.

"One hundred," the guard began to barter. Gerhard was adamant and shook his head vigorously. He had 'sized up' his customer.

"Two hundred or no watch," he said.

"Ok, ok! Give us the watch, and I'll bring the fags when I come on duty tonight."

Gerhard was not so daft. "Fags first, then watch," he said.

"Alright! You win! I'm back on duty at midnight, and I'll see you here in this same spot," and to emphasise his point, he pointed to his forefinger at the ground between his boots.

When he was sure that Gerhard understood, off he went with his last made contact, and if the guard really wanted his bloody watch, which incidentally did not work anyway, then he, Gerhard, could be having a smoke, the first in a long time, just after midnight tonight.

It was a moonlit night, and Gerhard crept silently towards the wire where the guard was waiting for him. "The cigarette?" he asked.

"The watch?" the guard parried.

Gerhard waved it towards him, and the exchange was made. He hoped they would go for at least ten minutes. He had spent the intervening time trying to tinker with it and wind it up just before he crept out of his tent!

For a few minutes, the guard was 'off guard!' and Gerhard of the S.S. was disgusted. What a guard! What a damn-awful soldier! And in a flash, the rifle was in Gerhard's hands. The Tommy whirled around, but too late. He froze as Gerhard slowly raised the rifle towards him. For a few seconds tension thickened the air between them. Gerhard's eyes gleamed, and for a minute he really was tempted. What was there to stop him shooting this miserable example of soldiery, and them making a run for it? He could do it! The guard was frankly terrified, making little sounds of fear in his throat, and holding his hands out in full view. Then Gerhard realised – one shot and the entire camp would be on him. And where could he go anyway, he didn't know where he was!

The guard began to speak, and his voice was squeaky with fright. "Give that back to me, you German swine, or I'll report you."

"Go on then," challenged Gerhard, "and how will you explain the loss of your rifle to your sergeant, eh? A fine guard you turned out to be."

He looked down at the rifle in his hands, and with practised ease, sought and removed the bolt. He weighed it thoughtfully in his hand. For a few seconds none of them spoke.

"I'll you what we do," Gerhard said. "You haf back rifle, and I keep zis. Tomorrow you have zis back for five hundred cigarettes."

"I can't get five hundred bloody fags," hissed the guard, his courage returning.

"You get them," said Gerhard in a soft and reasonable voice.

"You get them tomorrow. If not zis goes down the latrine, and is lost…"

The Guard capitulated. "OK. I'll get them when I go off duty. About two a.m."

"Good," said Gerhard, softly. "I come back then. This is no good to me, but you have trouble if they find you lost it?"

He threw the rifle back to the guard, and put the bolt over the wire, watching it fall at the feet of the guard. "There is always somebody somewhere," reflected Gerhard with unusual philosophy.

"Always one person on the make, wanting to trade. All you have to do is to look!"

And finding a comparatively quiet spot behind his tent, he sat down, and drew deeply and thankfully on the first of his cigarettes.

Next morning there was an early roll-call. Herbert was rudely awakened found it was barely dawn. "Mein Gott," he muttered, trying to force his eyelids to remain open, and scratching his head and belly at the same time. "Mein Gott! Why is it that they have to do everything at the crack of dawn? Why so bloody early? The days are long enough…"

They all lined up as usual, and the Tommies counted… and counted… and counted yet again. An hour passed, and they all remained standing. Then they started all over again, and counted them once more. Obviously there was something wrong or something was going to be wrong in a minute, Herbert could plainly see that. What the hell was the matter? He began to feel apprehensive. He had pins and needles in his leg, and he needed to go the lavatory!

Then the Tommies came down the line again, but very slowly this time, and every so often a prisoner was picked out, and made to stand in front of the line. "You," said the Tommy, and poked Herbert in the chest with his forefinger. Herbert stepped two paces in front as the others

31

had done, and waited. His heart was beating fast, and the hair on the back of his head began to itch! He looked sideways along the line from the corner of his eye and realised that all those who had been made to stand out had S.S. uniforms on. 'Christ!' he thought and began to sweat. Gerhard Schreiber stood near to him.

When the Tommies had sorted out all the S.S. to their satisfaction, the rest of the camp was dismissed. The S.S. prisoners were marched out of the gate in files of three, and under the guard of six British soldiers, were taken into a nearby wood. Herbert with his passion for order, had already counted the heads as they were hustled along, and he thought there was some thirty-five of them. The column was halted, and ordered to sit on the ground.

A British officer arrived in a car, closely followed by an army lorry, from which two other officers descended. The guards called the prisoners attention. One of the officers addressed them in fluent German.

"It has come to our notice," he said, "that the S.S. have on more than one occasion violated the Geneva Convention, and have misused, shamefully misused, the symbol of the Red Cross. They have used ambulances to take ammunition to the front lines, and thus have gained extra support, and inflicted casualties on our forces. You have been picked out from members of the same S.S. and are therefore guilty of such violation. You will face the death penalty! You will be shot!"

This lengthy explanation was received in total and stunned silence. Herbert felt the blood drain from his face. He had often read this phrase in books, but now he actually felt it happen, but he did not feel frightened.

He was rather surprised at his own reaction, but he honestly felt no fear at this moment. He felt nothing. Not numbed, resigned… nothing. All the confusion, the chaos and pain of the last few weeks, all the death and suffering… He felt nothing. The blood and corpses of his comrades, folded up awkwardly in death. The lined and tired faces of the old men, and unexpected small acts of bravery, like old Helmut dragging him out of the damned farmhouse. Helmut was hardly the hero type! And look at what he had done! He had saved Herbert, but not for long apparently, for now it was all about to end, and Herbert was to be shot! 'Poor old Helmut!' he thought, 'he wasted his bloody life.' He remembered young Hans, with the smooth unlined face and quiff of blonde hair falling into his eyes. They were all dead now. He felt almost relieved. At least he knew what was going to happen. He felt his tightened muscles slightly relax.

'This is the bloody end of it all, then', he reflected, and rather wished he could have written a note to someone, perhaps to his mother or brother.

The end of all the fighting, all the battles. All the bloody propaganda that everybody had been spouting. Finale! Finis! The finis of Herbert Baum-Hacker! Shot! Ignominiously, in an unidentified wood somewhere in France. What would they do with his body? Leave it here? Or would someone dig it up again years later, and wonder who he was? All these thoughts across his mind. Everybody seemed to be stunned, for no one has moved. No one had spoken.

"All strip," the guards shouted, coming along the line, and prodding with rifle butts to emphasise their own urgency. "All strip." Still silent, their column began to slowly obey. "Hande hoch," was the next command, and everybody immediately held their hands high above their heads. Once again the Tommies moved slowly along the line, slowly scrutinising each prisoner's skin.

'What the hell are they playing at?' Herbert thought wearily. 'If they are going to shoot us, who don't they bleeding well get on with it?'

Again, one or two of the prisoners were brought out to stand before one of the officers. Herbert's turn came. The officer looked beneath his arms. They were filthy and smelled abominably since water for washing was non-existent.

"Where's yours?" he bawled.

Herbert looked at him with total blankness.

"Where is it? Where is it?"

"Sir," said Herbert all at sea.

"Where is it? I thought you all had them here."

"Where is what, sir?"

"Your bloody S.S. tattoo mark, you German swine."

Enlightenment dawned upon Herbert, and the blank expression crept from his face. So that's what they were looking for. And, of course, he had been wearing an S.S. tunic.

"I don't belong to the S.S.," he said, standing to attention as best as he might.

"Well, why are you wearing this bloody tunic then?" the officer shouted, picking up Herbert's discarded garment, and thrusting it beneath his nose. "This is S.S. uniform isn't it?"

"Yes sir! But not mine. I was wounded before I got captured. I lost my tunic at a field dressing station, and had to grab hold of the first one that was around when they moved us out. It happened to be this one. I was not in the S.S. I was in the…"

"Wounded?

Where?"

"Right thigh," and Herbert, pointing to the thick blood encrusted wrapping around the top of his leg. The officer poked at it gingerly but appeared to be convinced. He told Herbert to stand out with four other prisoners, who had apparently managed to convince the officer that they were not members of the S.S.

The other prisoners were loaded into the lorry, and driven away, while Herbert's small group were marched back to the camp. And they marched. In the near distance, they heard a few bursts of machine gun fire, but nobody said anything, and nobody asked any questions. There was total silence, except for the sound of their feet touching the ground in unison.

As he entered the tent, Herbert caught sight of Gerhard's cigarettes, the ones that he had traded with the guard for. They were tucked beneath his blanket, and they stayed there. Nobody touched them, and nobody smoked them. It was as if the interlude never happened, for it was never mentioned, nor referred to again, even obliquely. But everybody knew about it.

Morale in the camp was low. The more or less constant hunger, lack of food, lack of news, and uncertainty was getting to them all. The incident in the wood seemed to be a finishing touch.

Three weeks later, they were again on the move, loaded on to lorries driven rapidly towards the coast ready for shipment. The drive was, as usual, a nightmare. The roads ploughed up by shells and tanks were incredible, and Herbert was convinced that the drivers used for the transporting of prisoners must be handpicked. There was not a single pot hole that they did not descend into; not a single bump that they did not drive over at a great speed. The men in the back were thrown side to side, and jerked backwards and forwards with every mile they covered.

When they reached the coast, Herbert looked with interest at the 'prison' ship. It was basically enormous square iron box, with floors, walls and ceiling of steel. It had no windows, only very small round portholes very high up so that no one was able to see out of them, and they would only let in the minimal amount of fresh air. Rumours, as usual, abounded. The prisoners were slightly heartened by the move, and were curious to know where they were being taken. It could be Canada? Perhaps New Zealand or Australia? They were all parts of the British Empire, weren't they? Herbert thought he wouldn't mind having a look around Canada or somewhere, but he hoped they would not be taken that far afield in such a vessel. Anyway, what did it matter what they wanted? They were prisoners and would have to go wherever they were taken.

Twelve cardboard boxes came into the hold after, the prisoners were installed, and seven lavatory buckets. "Thank God for that at least," Herbert said.

Slowly, the boarding ramp was winched up and every vestige of daylight, and every sound slowly faded from eye to ear. Five hundred or so prisoners were enclosed in this huge floating iron box. Nobody actually seemed to suffer from technical claustrophobia, but as the last crack of daylight disappeared from the top of the boarding ramp, a little rustle of panic rippled fitfully among them. Herbert looked down at his feet. Between them was a bolt hole and in dimness he could just see, by the shine, that it was full of water. He watched it move from side to side. They were afloat. They had embarked. "We're off!" he said aloud.

The cardboard boxes were found to contain the inevitable, and by this time totally unsatisfying bully beef and dry biscuits. Again! The lavatory buckets soon reached overflowing, and the smell in the close confinement of the hold was indescribable! A few of the men, undernourished and debilitated, began to feel sea sick, moaned a little, and then vomited with some difficulty, retching painfully with their thick sounds.

The journey seemed never-ending, and they were all thankful to feel the great iron thing stop moving, and to hear the loading ramp being lowered again. Daylight gradually filtered back into the hold, and everyone pressed forward to take their first glimpse of the unknown. And draw the fresh air in great gulps.

Herbert's eyes looked around, and he discovered that they were in harbour somewhere. He spotted a familiar figure. Dark blue uniform, gleam of shiny silver buttons, pointed helmet? It was an English bobby! It was familiar to them all because of pictures in almost forgotten school books. He had never seen one before. A real English bobby, fairly rotund, and avuncular. They were in England!

Chapter III:

Dockside to Yorkshire

After disembarking the prisoners under heavy guard, the march through the town began. It was the first time that most of them had set foot on English soil, and although they still felt very wobbly after the long hours at sea, they looked about them with curiosity, and despite their unkempt appearance, and haggard faces, they felt their spirits lift, just slightly.

Herbert took a childlike delight in spotting the English bobbies that seemed familiar. The buildings looked much the same as in any other town, almost anywhere in the world, but it seemed strange to see traffic moving on the 'wrong' side of the street. There were goods in the shop windows, and whole town seemed alive and busy.

Why 'they' thought it was necessary to provide such a heavy guard was a mystery to Herbert, more so now the miles of the English Channel lay between them and their homeland. Nobody but an absolute fool would want to get into the fighting again, even if they thought for one moment there was a remote possibility. He certainly didn't! By God, no. He was ,by his very nature, a peaceful man, and he did not take kindly to excitement, upheaval, and a general lack of organisation. And he felt bone weary. He had seen enough of war to last him one lifetime, and he had narrowly escaped death on two occasions within the past few weeks.

He was glad that the Grim Reaper had seen fit to pass him by, but now, all he wanted was to be able to sit down somewhere, to stop moving around, to settle in one place, and collect his thoughts which were still very confused. He did not want to bother with anything or anybody. He just wanted to sit still and wait until it was time to go home. He thought that, when peace came, perhaps he could retire, for a while at least, lie under a tree, and let peace wash over him, like a wave washing over a shore.

As they marched through the town, some with dragging steps, the civilians watched them with overt curiosity, and some showed real hostility, their faces becoming tight, enclosed, and their eyes hard. This, more than anything yet, made Herbert realise how vulnerable they were, for this was indeed their enemy's country, and these the enemy's own people. He thought he understood. He tried to imagine just how he would feel if the positions had been reversed, and he had witnessed British prisoners of war being marched through his home town of Hamburg. God knows!

Food was rationed over here, and he knew there were shortages, and now there were all these bloody Germans to be fed as well. Of course, there was resentment, and antipathy. No wonder they stared at the moving column of filthy, ragged, thin, hollow-eyed, 'enemies' with hostility.

The march continued until they came to what was obviously a military camp, and at the entrance Herbert read the sign 'Delousing Centre' written in English and German.

'Thank God,' he thought.

Personal hygiene had been at a minimum ever since they had been captured, and he, and all the others, were aware of the fact that they had lice, since they had been unable to wash, or take off their clothes for weeks.

They had fantasies about large white baths filled with hot soapy water from which steam rose in clouds of vapour, followed by a brisk rub down with warm thick white towels. Of nail brushes, and back brushes, and endless, endless water. Of freshly laundered clothes and clean underwear.

The wound in Herbert's thigh was now almost healed over, but he thought of the delightful soothing effect it would have on the tightening skin if he could wash it in a tub. He had always been fastidious, and very particular about his personal appearance, and now his too-long hair, bodily dirt, and the presence of lice in his clothing and the need to scratch, all filled him with abhorrence and made his present situation almost untenable.

In single file they entered the barracks. "Haircut," was the first order, and everybody breathed a sigh of relief. On this day, most of them looked a sorry sight. Then they realised this was no ordinary haircut. Not a decent short back and sides, but a 'bolsh' – 'all off.' No one was immune. No one was consulted, officer, sergeant, or private, they had no special treatment. 'All off' for everybody.

Herbert wondered what these barbers had done for a living in civilian life, for it was a certain fact that they had not been engaged in cutting hair. Their work did not reach anything near a professional level, and heaven alone knew where they had been fetched from, but they hacked away with ill-concealed delight, and an unbelievable ham-fistedness, until everyone had a short head, a red bullet cut, covered with greyish bristle, and showing up every phrenological bump on their encrusted skulls.

The next order was one that was the beginning to sound a bit too familiar. "Strip! Everybody strip!"

'Bloody hell,' Herbert thought silently. 'Surely they are not going to make another search for the S.S. tattoo number?'

They were instructed to throw their uniforms away on to a heap, and it was with some relief that they were able to rid themselves of their filthy clothing. As Herbert threw what was left of his uniform on to the growing pile, the actions seemed to him to be symbolic: the end of the link from home. He was here, standing naked in the land of the enemy, with no possessions left at all, for now everything had been taken from him, and he was left owning nothing. Even his tattered uniform belonged to the past; the final link seemed to have been severed.

The end of the German army. He felt a strange shiver in the area of his spine, and this came not only from the cold.

He felt vulnerable alone in this crowd, in a way which he could not fully understand.

The prisoners were then told to stand in single file, and large flat wooden box was placed in position. One by one they were instructed to stand upon it, and they raised their arms high above their heads. A British soldier, with a syringe at least two feet long, and full of DDT delousing powder, skilfully squirted everybody from top to bottom, fore and aft, making sure that the powder entered into every wrinkle and fold of skin. There seemed to be little chance that any 'lodgers' could survive after that.

After the powder blast, and the coughing and spluttering with eyes streaming, the prisoners walked on to the next stage of the delousing operation: the shower rooms. They were really looking forward to this, the first thing approaching a bath that any of them had experienced for weeks. A real bath – warm water? Soap? And their skin able to breathe again! They surged forward. Inside the shower room were four long pipes along the ceiling with holes drilled into them at regular intervals. They looked upward, as men look towards heaven for manna, their eyes still smarting from DDT, but all that emerged from each hole was a thin trickle of tepid water.

To actually get wet all over was going to be hard labour, and the men, literally streaked and daubed with greyish rapidly caking powder, elbowed each other aside in a frantic effort to get clean.

The pushing and shoving was fairly good-natured, and the concrete floor was wetter than the prisoners, until the sound of the slapping of wet and bare feet on the rivulets of water added to the general din.

To Herbert, as he watched, the sight was a comic one, but a sad one too. This was the German army, jumping around, stark naked. Thin ones, short ones, long and fat ones, flabby flesh and all, with thin rivers of water making patterns like tear marks down the grey dust that covered them from head to foot.

One short, stocky, belligerent sort of chap elbowed his way in.

"Move over, fatty," he said, and there was an edge of malice in the tone of his voice.

"Are you addressing me, soldier?" replied 'Fatty.'

"Stand to attention, man! I am an officer, and I shall have you on report."

"Get stuffed," said the little 'un tartly. "Officer, eh? You're now no better than the rest of us. We're all in the same boat here. Prisoners of bloody war, and if it hadn't been for the likes of you lot, us lot wouldn't bloody well be here."

His eyes gleamed, and raising his dust caked arm, he emphasised each word with a jab of the forefinger in 'Fatty's' guts.

"Take a tip mate," he continued. "Learn a lesson! Come off your high horse and sweat it out with the rest of us. Neither you, nor nobody else gets preferential treatment here. Not from us, and not from them. Right?"

'Fatty' seemed to swell with rage. He visibly inflated, and his cheeks distended. He stood straight, his legs stiff, his whole stance reminiscent of a parade ground, but the effect ruined by his fat belly, thin thighs and flabby genitals.

"Your name and rank, soldier?" he bawled, opening his mouth wide, "I demand to know."

Little 'un looked him up and down with a ponderous sarcasm and said, "Oh! You mean I didn't tell you? Private Churchill, and Winston is my uncle! I shall probably be having tea with him this afternoon," and he minced a few yards off, then whipping around and changing his tone, "Look mate! Bloody lay off! The war is over... finished. Can't you get that into your fat skull? It's finished... all over. For all of us. We're all in the same bleeding boat! So, don't give me any more of your bleeding orders..." And he strode swiftly out of the room without even getting wet.

'Christ' though Herbert. 'Are we to go on like this for… how long? Officers! Orders! The bloody war, and who should have done that…? All this time, two silly bastards have to start it up all over again… Christ!'

He finished his meagre shower, managed to get all of the DDT out of his mouth and eyes, and rubbed himself down with a soaking wet bit of towelling left on the end of the bench.

Again, they were ordered to form a single file, and run to the next hut, about twenty yards away, where clean clothing was to be issued. Here trestle tables were piled high with assorted bits of German uniforms. Each prisoner had an item of clothing thrusted towards them indiscriminately, with no attempt to check the size, until every man had one of everything available. They all had been cleaned but some of them were so badly shrunk that it is doubtful if they would have fitted a child. Again, they stood outside, shivering slightly from the cool shower, and clutching their armful of assorted clothing.

Herbert found himself in possession of a sock which had more holes in it than actual feet, a pair of green drill trousers, and an infantry jacket that hung down well below the tips of his fingers and sloped off his shoulders. He looked around at his fellow prisoners. 'God what a Charlie Chaplin outfit,' he thought. 'Still, who cares now?'

Permission was given to swap around, and eventually everyone was dressed in something. No distinction was made between officers and other ranks at this stage, and there was some grumbling at this.

Then followed the best thing that had happened to Herbert in weeks. They were issued with a hot meal, and this was the first hot cooked meal they had been given since their capture. It was beans and potatoes with gravy, and a chunk of white bread. It tasted good. In fact, it tasted bloody marvellous, and Herbert could not remember a more welcoming meal. He savoured the white bread and gravy, mopping the plate clean until no trace remained.

Never, he thought, had he enjoyed anything more than this. And at the same time, the little man inside his head noted with amazement that there should come a time when a simple meal of bread, potatoes and gravy should seem like luxury. Herbert was a man of a hearty appetite which seldom, if ever failed him.

His mother had been an excellent cook, and he thought with longing of the family meals 'before the war'. He had always been able to put away substantial helpings of everything without the slightest effect, and without putting on an ounce of extra weight. But that, of course, was in another world.

Sometimes it seemed to him, when he looked back, it was as if he were looking at a toy theatre, and all his family were little coloured cardboard characters, moving around stiffly, on little sticks, and not real people at all. Was it really like that? Did they all really sit, and eat, and chatter to each other like this? Did they have no inkling that this holocaust was only around the corner, ready to engulf them? He thrusted the thought away from him.

Casually he wondered if there was any chance of a second helping. There wasn't.

Again, under heavy guard, they left the camp, marched back through the town, following a similar route to their first one, and then to the railway station, where they put into carriages coupled to the rear of a goods train. The usual checks were made, doors and windows were locked, and the train started on its slow, inexorable, chugging journey.

Herbert, ever cautious, had played safe. He had kept a quarter of his chunk of bread in his pocket. He didn't quite know why, since he had been hungry enough, but it seemed a good idea at the time.

'You never know how long it will be until they give anything else,' he thought, and the habit of conservation which had stemmed from the issue of six dry biscuits a day, and his earnest and fruitless attempts to save up enough to 'have a feast' remained with him.

The movement of the train was somewhat soporific, and as Herbert drowsed, he reflected that he could accept, and put up with being defeated, with being a prisoner. He could even, at a pinch, put up with being dirty, unkempt and lousy. If he was forced to, he could put up with being cold. But he could never put up with being hungry again; not if there was anything he could do about it. It was worse than fear. It was not merely the question of having an empty stomach, of not being fed, it went much further than that. It was totally lowering, both morally and physically. It drained the body of all desire for movement, it prevented all clarity of thought, the feeling of hunger entirely dominating one's whole existence until there seemed to be nothing else in the world but the desire of food. It did more harm, Herbert thought, than a hail of enemy bullets… he was not going to be hungry again, he'd make damned sure about that.

The train chugged steadily through the English countryside, and Herbert who had managed to get a seat by the window, had his first glimpse of his enemy's homeland. He thought that it was ironic really. In the German army he had done a great deal of walking. He had marched mile after mile. Now, since he had been taken prisoner, he had been carried everywhere.

In a mild sort of way, he began to enjoy this journey. One thing resolved. He had been brought to England against his will, a prisoner to be locked in, and locked up. But now he was here, he would derive as much benefit from all of it as he could. Herbert the fatalist. Herbert who would always take whatever the Gods dished out, and make it seem like it was what he had always wanted, make the best and most of it.

He had never before had any opportunity for foreign travel, and this was hardly what he would have chosen anyway, but this seemingly was the way it had to be, so Herbert would see, and learn as much as he could. The train steamed gently northwards, and guards patrolled the corridors. Herbert fell asleep, his head lolling gently upon the hairy upholstery of the carriage.

He was rudely awakened when the train halted to a sharp jerk which threw him forward. 'Bloody hell,' he thought, and put out an arm to save himself.

"Where are we?" asked a chap called Kurt, sitting next to Herbert.

"Still in England, you fool. Where else?"

The familiar cry echoed around the train. "Alles Raus! Mag Schnell! Come on… Come on…"

It was dark outside, and Herbert peered around him, trying to see the name of the place written somewhere, but all the nameplates on railway stations had long been removed. This was so that German paratroopers would be confused, and not know where they landed! He learned this later, and thought it was very funny.

All along the train, prisoners were stumbling out, stretching and yawning after the tedious journey. The guard rattled up and down. "Come on you bloody lot of Hitlers!" he shouted and lined them all up, at least to his own satisfaction, on the platform. It had started to rain.

It took them half an hour to march to their headquarters, and by that time, the rain has soaked right through. Another wire compound, full of tents. Herbert sighed. It all looked so familiar.

'Back to square one,' he thought. Once inside the wire, there was a quick roll-call to make sure that nobody had gone missing on the journey, although how on earth this could have been accomplished, and where they would have escaped to, was beyond Herbert's comprehension. Then they were all dismissed and instructed to find somewhere to sleep for the night.

Someone mentioned food, but there was none to be had. Herbert remembered the cube of bread in his pocket. It was none too clean, and there was a few bits fluff adhering to it, but he didn't care. It was better than nothing, so he blew on it, wiped it off on his sleeve, and began to eat it, very slowly, nibbling his front teeth like a rabbit, so as to make it last that bit longer.

He had got about halfway through when he noticed that the chap sitting next to him was watching his every move. "Where the hell did you scrounge that from?" he asked.

"I suppose you ate all yours back at the camp?" Herbert said, wearily.

"Too true. I did, mate. I was bloody starving. I still am," the chap sighed, and leaned back, closing his eyes. Herbert looked ruefully at the remaining two inches of bread. It was his; he could have saved some of his own, couldn't he? But the pleasure had gone from his meagre feast, and Hebert, looking at the gaunt young face, relented.

"Here," he said, "You can have the last bit."

The soldier grabbed it. "Thanks mate. That's bloody good of you. Sure you can spare it?" and without waiting for Herbert's reply, he wolfed it down.

Still hungry, Herbert slept. When morning came, nothing at first seemed to be happening, except that it was still raining. It was a thin greyish sort of miserable sort of rain. He looked about him. Twelve men in one tent, all facing the centre, with their feet around the pole, all fitting neatly together, just like a can of sardines. He swiftly wrenched his thoughts from sardines! Their makeshift clothing was still clammy from their soaking of the previous night, and the wet wool smelled slightly.

Herbert rose to his feet and stuck his head outside. There seemed to be around a hundred tents contained in the compound; he thought it looked like another transit camp, and not a permanent billet. This meant that they would in all possibility be on the move again fairly soon.

Suddenly, the order for the roll-call belched forth from the loudspeaker system. Everyone began moving, and there came sounds of desperate activity from the nearby latrine block. As Herbert watched, a little fat infantryman came running out, hauling on his trousers as he ran.

"I'm sick of roll-call, bloody roll-call," he shouted as he caught up with Herbert.

"I got a bit of a stomach problem... you know? Lack of food, I suppose. It always catches me like this, and I go in there for a quiet sit down... on my own... troubling nobody. But will they leave you alone? No, they bloody won't. No, I've been cut off, and I shall have to go back and start all over again... it's not right, you know. They shouldn't do this!" Herbert looked at him in amazement. Was this all he had been worrying about?

People were dead, houses bombed, they were all hungry, and locked up behind barbed wire... and all he was bothered about was going to the lavatory. Christ!

"I'm going to make an official complaint," the man continued, his voice raised is agitation. "I shall make a complaint. Have you any idea where I can go to do this?" Herbert was disgusted. The man didn't seem to understand.

"Do you honestly think anybody's going to take any notice of your complaint?" he asked. "Do you think for a minute anyone gives a damn? You are a prisoner! You are an alien, an enemy. They have got us. We are defeated, and they can do what the hell they like! A prisoner, get it? For just as long as they would like to keep you. No, do what the bloody hell you like," and he left the chap, red-faced and angry, tucking his shirt into the depths of his trousers.

Once again, they stood in ranks of three, and were counted. Herbert standing to attention, attempted to look up and down the line from the corner of his eyes, and suddenly he almost shouted aloud. It was not possible, was it? After all this he could not believe it. He spotted a face that he thought he knew... but he told himself to wait and see.

With ill-concealed impatience, Herbert waited for the order to dismiss, and turned his head. Only a few yards away from him stood his old schoolmate, Erwin Fieldhouse. It was him, Herbert was sure, although he had not seen him in years. He lived only two doors away from him in Hamburg, but somehow, with them both being away in the army, and their few leaves never seeming to coincide, they had rather lost touch with each other. But it was Erwin, and now to see him here, in these conditions...

It would be difficult to say which of these two was the more astonished. Erwin's face lit up with a round grin. For a moment, they did not speak, but just thumped each other on the back. At length, Erwin said, "What about the Führer and the Third Reich now, Herbert, my friend? Things no longer look good for us..."

"For God's sake, don't start talking about the war..." Herbert said. "I don't know how I feel. I don't know anything. And it would be take far too long... But I'm damn glad to see you..."

"How long have you been here?"

"When were you captured?"

"What happened to your lot?"

The inevitable questions flew thick and fast between them. Erwin had been with a Panzer Regiment and had been captured only about three weeks before Herbert. He said he never quite knew how it all happened. Everything was going well, and suddenly the allies had landed, and from then on, it was retreat and chaos. Their orders had meant nothing and had been impossible to carry out. Then one night, he found himself completely surrounded by the enemy, and had been taken prisoner. Personally, it had come as a relief... in a way. He was damn well glad to be out of it.

"I wonder how long we are to stay here," Herbert said.

"I suppose it's another transit camp. I hope it is. We only came in two days ago," said Erwin, "and I think all of us are on the move, perhaps even today. At least that's what I heard from one of the guards!"

Herbert wondered silently if there was any chance of them staying together. It was good to see Erwin again, a very real link with home. Their real home in Hamburg.

They had been friends when they were younger, and there were many happy memories they could share.

They ambled slowly around the compound together, and Erwin was obviously thinking along the same lines. "I wish we could stay together, old mate," he said. "You and I sit out this war together, here in England. It can't last all that much longer, and then I suppose we shall go home again. But it would be nice to have someone to talk to? You remember how we used to talk and talk in the old days. For hours we talked… far into the night?"

He nodded remembering. He also remembered how they had argued! Erwin was rather a forceful character and didn't like it when people disagreed with him.

"Well! Keep your fingers crossed! Stranger things have been known to happen," he said.

He felt that if he and Erwin should be sent to the same camp, it would be better for both of them. They could talk of people and things familiar to both of them, and then things would not be so totally alien. He would not feel so completely lost. There were times, not often, but occasionally, and Herbert never spoke of them to anyone, where he felt so remote from all he had ever known, from all those he held in affection, from all familiar things, that he had slight feelings of panic. For all he knew, everybody did, but no one ever mentioned it. All the prisoners presented a reasonably cheerful face to each other. It was part of the unwritten code! Morale! It was supposed to help keep spirits up. But there were still the watches of the night!

There was such a terrible lack of news! None of them had heard from home for a long time. They had been on the move amidst all the fighting, so no mail could possibly have reached them there. Any letters must have been lost, and they had no means of finding out what was happening to their families. Nor could they be sure that they had not been posted as missing or dead.

They had no idea what was going to happen to them. It was obvious that they were going to be taken somewhere else, but where? And for what?

Herbert and Erwin, and indeed all the others had been fighting the British. The British were pigs, weren't they? They had been told so often enough. Now they were prisoners in the hands of the British, and how could they know what would happen to them? What sort of treatment would they get?

Anything could be in store for them. So far, they had received no ill usage whatsoever. True, they were hungry. And some of them could have done with slightly warmer clothing. But, food was scarce, and was rationed. Clothing too was rationed, so they did not really expect to live like kings.

Herbert and Erwin were thoughtful as they shook hands upon parting to return to their different tents, and they both hoped that they would end up in the same hut when the prisoners were all moved on.

Three hours later, the entire camp was once again standing to attention. Form up in ranks, be counted, and then begin to march through the town to the railway station. Loaded into carriages, doors and windows were securely locked, and at the given signal, the train began to move, chugging away, picking up speed as it went. 'What a bloody waste of time,' Herbert thought. 'All this way, and just for one night, and a wet arse into the bargain. Now it looks as though we are heading back the way we came…' and it was raining again.

Herbert could not get the meeting with Erwin out of his mind. How good it had been to see him again, to come face-to-face like that. A chance in a million. Miles from home in enemy territory, and there was old Erwin, large as life. It would be great if they could stay together, even just in the same camp. But all that was in the lap of the gods.

Erwin was a great chap, Herbert reflected, and it was good to know that he was safe and well anyway. If he got the chance to write home at all, he would mention to his mother that he had run across him, and his mother could then slip round and tell Erwin's parents. That would please them all! He had a mental picture of his mother, sitting down and drinking a cup of coffee (ersatz of course) with Mrs Fieldhouse, while they talked about them. He clung to this comfortable image, and resolutely pushed aside intruding visions of bombed buildings, heaps of rubble, and injured civilians.

He wouldn't think about it! He would just think about his mother and Mrs Fieldhouse! As soon as ever he could, as soon as he was allowed to do so… if he was… if he could write home and let them all know he was safe. Both he and Erwin.

Chapter IV:

Transit Camp in Wales

Their new destination, Transit Camp 17, lay somewhere in the middle of Wales, surrounded by the looming greyish-green hummocks of the Welsh mountains. Upon arrival, Herbert looked around him with his customary curiosity and interest but found the scenery somewhat uninspiring. The day was a grey one, and the heads of the mountains were obscured by swirling clouds, and the general feeling was one of being 'shut in'. There was no 'vista', no 'view' and the countryside had vaguely submissive appearance.

The train journey had, as usual, been slow and halting, and they were all longing for a drink, their throats dry in the warm dusty atmosphere of the locked carriages. Herbert allowed his mind to dwell with some longing upon a mug of hot tea, and while he was about it, he thought he would give himself a treat, and allow it to dwell upon the thought of food, as well as drink.

This camp was surrounded by at least eight-feet of barbed wire, and once again, as before, all the prisoners were subjected to a thorough search before being allowed to enter. A tall thin Tommy was doing most of the searching, and he grinned as Herbert stood in front of him, arms stretched out. The soldier patted him all over and looked at him sideways out of the corner of his eye. 'Carry on mate' Herbert thought, 'you'll find damn all on me. Even if I had anything, somebody else would have found it before now!'

When the search was completed, they were allowed to enter the Camp, and once inside, the other German POWs came forward and subjected the newcomers to severe scrutiny, searching their faces, hoping to see someone they knew, or someone from their own former unit, someone with some news. But it didn't often work out that way; each group was just as confused as the other.

The new arrivals were assembled and marched to the hut of the Lagerführer (German camp commandant) which stood in the centre of the compound. A fat little major of the German artillery, strutting with self-importance, bustled about as they lined up, and then he addressed then, still marching affectedly up and down, his hands clasped loosely behind his back.

"I am Major Koller, your camp commandant," he said, and paused for a minute to let this fantastic piece of information sink in.

"You have been brought to Camp 17 for the time being. I don't know how long. I hope you will find life here not too unpleasant, we try…" with a deprecating wave of his fat white hand, "… we try and make the best of things now we are all together in captivity. I hope that every one of you will abide by our camp rules. Order and discipline must be maintained at all times. Some of us have been here for quite some time, and I do not wish that any of you will disrupt the smooth running of this camp."

Here the major's voice began to rise shrilly, and he brought it down an octave with difficulty. He swallowed. "Our relations with the British are, in fact quite good, and I want it to stay that way. If any of you have any ideas about escape, I insist you forget about it immediately. The camp is patrolled twenty-four hours a day, inside and outside, so any funny business about digging tunnels, or breaking out, would be discovered immediately. So again, I tell you to forget it. That's all I have to say to you at this stage."

Herbert was incensed by this 'welcome' speech by the Major like nothing else so far.

"The bloody little creep," he muttered. "The bloody little creep! Right up the Tommy's arse. You're alright, Jack! I bet he's got a real soft billet here. Got everything lined up… And all he had to do in return, is to keep us poor sods in order! No wonder he wants to keep the rules. It would upset his little applecart if we stepped out of line. Now wouldn't that be a pity. The jumped up little pipsqueak!"

He swallowed the bile that had risen in his throat at the major's speech.

"Shut up and keep calm, Herbert," he told himself. "Play it by the ear, my lad. Play it by the ear! At least this looks like a proper camp, and a damn sight more inviting than the wet bell tents of the last one. Shut up and keep your nose clean!"

Herbert was allocated to Hut No.28 which looked exactly like all the others, and like them, contained twenty-five double bunk beds. With his infallible instinct for self-preservation, he managed to get hold of a top bunk at the far end, which his experience suggested would be the warmest place and less likely to catch any droughts when the door opened. He would have preferred the bottom bunk, but the chap with him was much older than Herbert, about fifty-five in fact, and he looked and seemed much older than his years. He seemed almost at the end of his tether, and Herbert offered him the bottom bunk so that he would not have to clamber about to get in.

Each bunk had a mattress filled with straw, two blankets and a hard pillow. Not exactly palatial, Herbert reflected, but a damn slight better than sleeping in dirty clothes on wet grass. There was a proper roof over their heads, and whether it rained or snowed, they would at least be sheltered.

He had slept in far worse conditions than this, even before he was captured. Just so long as 'they' didn't come tomorrow and move everyone on again. He was getting bloody fed up of all this aimless moving around. Perhaps 'they' would let them stay here for a bit, and get really settled in. After all, he had a lot of sleep to catch up on, and he was more than willing to start right now.

"Baum-Hacker Herbert," he introduced himself to his bunk-mate.

"Karl Geller from Dresden," and they shook hands. Rather formal really considering the circumstances, but the

German soldier is not one to drop the polite formalities. "This is a bit of a four-star as far as prison camps go," Herbert said, as they sat on Geller's bunk. Geller shrugged, and they chatted desultorily. Herbert had visited Dresden a couple of times, and it made a point of contact. The conversation at this stage was purely superficial, but even so, Herbert thought it was quite pleasant. He was, by nature, gregarious. He liked talking to people, and people he had not met before. He unwittingly filed away inside his head little anecdotes, tenuous connections, new jargon and phrases he would later be able to trot out should the need arise. Time at least was one commodity they had plenty of, and they both began to feel more comfortable and relaxed.

Suddenly over the loudspeaker, came the inevitable order, "Roll-call! Roll-call!"

Herbert and Geller looked resignedly at each other. "It's all the bloody time, isn't it?" said Geller.

"Here we go again…" and they went.

After roll-call, they had their first meal in this camp. Two men from each hut were detailed, on a rota system, to collect food from the canteen, and off they went, whilst everyone else waited for the ill-concealed impatience for their return. Ten loaves of bread, a can of black tea, and a tin of marmalade. This was to feed all fifty prisoners. With the innate German love of order, it was apportioned out with mathematical exactitude, and each man wolfed his share down ravenously.

It was not what they had expected, although they hardly expected anything. But when you are hungry, you make do with whatever there is, and at least the hot tea was very refreshing. Herbert felt revived, and his spirits lifted. Perhaps things were really getting a bit more organised now. There seemed to be reasonable arrangements for the distribution of food, and he found himself thinking a great deal about the distribution of food, these days. Despite of all his very real efforts to channel his thoughts into less evocative spheres, when he was deliberately trying to think about other things, or perhaps trying not to think at all, and make his mind a total blank, a mental picture of meat and gravy, with perhaps a few sliced onions mixed in somewhere, would float gently across the screen behind his eyes. Even toast! Hot and squelchy with butter, and some of that black cherry preserve they had at home sometimes. Or an apple pie!

His mother made a very good apple pie. Layers of apple, sliced with a little lemon juice, and some raisins, and the crust crisp and golden brown.

Uncle Friedrich lived in the country, a few miles outside of Hamburg, and when they were children, Herbert and Fritz would be taken to visit him often. Particularly in the autumn, he remembered, for Uncle Friedrich lived in an old house, with an orchard, and they would return from such visits with apples and pears. For a moment, he felt the almost physical sensation of biting into one of these pears now.

He wrenched his thoughts away from the aspect of juicy fruit, and thought about Uncle Friedrich. He had seemed so old to the child Herbert, but he had not been much older than Herbert's own mother. Where was Uncle Friedrich now, he wondered. And Aunt Elsa, his little 'cottage loaf' wife, who had been so kind to him and to Fritz, even allowing them to play with one of her most treasured possessions, a little carved box that played a tune when you opened the lid, and which would normally be kept in the highest polished sacrosanct front parlour. He had not heard anything of them for some years now. Were they still in that old house, picking fruit from the trees in the orchard? Or had this endless bloody war engulfed them too? He resolutely forced his thoughts away from the past, and into the future.

He wondered what had happened to Erwin. He had not seen him since they arrived here, and for all he knew he might have been sent on somewhere else. Perhaps he should stroll around the compound, and see if he could run into him somewhere, but judging by the roll-call, there was something like two thousand prisoners here, so finding him would not be easy.

He thrusted his hands deep into his pockets and wandered off. This was, he reflected, what the British called an 'evening constitutional', this aimless sort of strolling. They considered that it was 'good for you' so perhaps it would be good for him. He had better be careful though, for too much exercise would make him even hungrier than he already was.

He had almost decided that Erwin could not be at the camp, when suddenly there he was, right in front of him. "Christ! There you are, Herbert!" he shouted, waving his arms frantically. "I've been looking all over for you…"

"Alright! Calm down! You've found me!" Herbert's tone was placid.

"I've been shoved into Hut .52 with a right bloody shower," Erwin went on. "I don't understand a word they say, honest! They all seem to have come from Bavaria or some outlandish place, and their dialect… It's unbelievable. They might be talking Greek for all I know. Is there a spare bunk in your hut so I could be transferred?"

"No! We are full up," Herbert said, "but we only just got here after all. We shall just have to get used to things. It's a bit early to start trying to swap berths. Leave it for a bit, and let's see how it goes. We can meet and talk in the daytime and bloody hell, at night we shall be asleep anyway. Things will work out! We shall all have to make sure they work out. We could be here for a long time or not, we don't know. So, it's up to us really…"

"You're always so bloody practical! So God damn sensible!" Erwin spat out of his mouth.

"Why don't you explode sometimes, like all the rest of us? Put your fist through a window? Hit out at someone?"

Herbert rubbed his chin reflectively. "I don't know," he said, "I think I've had enough of the physical fist stuff to last me. I don't want to hit anybody. I never did. All I really wish is that we could turn the clock back a few years, and I know I can't do that. None of us can. So I'll just do the best I can – and wait to go home. If home is still there!"

Erwin thumped on the back. "Oh Christ! Come on," he said.

"Let's walk around the bleeding compound just once more, then we'll turn in."

Herbert suddenly remembered a girl they had both had once. What on earth was her name? Rather plump, she was, with fair hair and freckles across the bridge of her nose! Erwin had not known that Herbert was taking her on his motorcycle three nights of the week, while Erwin took her on the other three. What she did on the seventh night, they never did find out. Gerda! That was her name. Gerda Stahl! God, what a piece she was. A real 'hot-arse' she was. Herbert and Erwin had almost fallen out over her, because somehow Herbert had his days mixed up and roared up on his motorcycle, just in time to see Erwin and Gerda getting onto a bus! That ended the triangle!

Try as he might, Herbert could never get it out of Erwin how far he had got with Gerda. Whether she was just a one-night stand (or more literally, a three-night stand) or whether he had really thought of her seriously. It had bothered him for a while, until he realised that he had done Erwin a good turn by putting him off Gerda. She had only been good for a roll in the hay. Or the woods just outside of town. Gerda was anyone's for a bit of fun, a night out and a cheap bit of jewellery! At the time he had known her, she was a 'well-meaning amateur' (the army's polite phraseology), but even then she was well on the way to turning professional! The oldest game in the world. Alright to play, but… one does not marry into it!

"Here Erwin, do you remember Gerda Stahl?" he said.

For a moment Erwin looked vague. Then "Oh! Gerda!" and he laughed.

"What a little bitch she was. My first, I think. They say you remember the first best, don't they? I did you a favour there, my friend. You had a narrow escape!"

58

"Me! Don't be so daft! I was never in the danger zone, mate," Herbert was quite indignant. "I thought I had upset everything for you…" and they laughed together.

Herbert thought how precious laughter was in these days. How good it felt to laugh with Erwin over this stupid incident in their joint past. How long ago it seemed and how trivial. Yet here they were, two war-weary veterans, in an alien country, locked in a prison compound, able to laugh over it.

Well perhaps things were not so bad after all, they told each other. They were fed. Not lavishly, it is true, but just about adequately. They had warm clothes. Okay, so they did not fit, only where they touched, but they kept them reasonably warm. They had a bed and a roof over all. They even had guards constantly patrolling them to make sure that no harm befell them. Surely, they could put up with all this until it was time for them to go home?

Herbert and Erwin said goodnight, and returned to their respective huts. Herbert clambered into his top bunk. Below him, Geller stirred in his sleep, and grunted. The pillow was rather hard, and it took him a few minutes to wriggle himself a dent in the straw of the mattress. But then, in no time at all, or so it seemed, he was warm and comfortable. He pulled the hair greyish blanket right up to his chin, his eyelids grew heavy, and the blessed oblivion of sleep swept over him.

In the next few days, the whole camp seemed to fall into the regularity of routine so beloved by the Germans, and by Herbert in particular. He disliked lack of organisation more than anything; in fact, he had little patience with it, for he was himself fairly good at establishing a routine, writing things down, apportioning things out, and making sure that everybody knew what they were expected to do, and exactly when. In a comparatively short period of time, it appeared they have been living in this camp almost forever.

One morning, after roll-call, he ran full-pelt, literally into Geller, who had been walking round and round the hut, with a face as long as a fortnight of wet Fridays. Herbert stopped dead, and looked hard at him. Poor old Geller! It was obvious that there was something wrong.

"What the hell's up with you, mate?" Herbert's tone was kindly.

"I've got a blasted toothache, that's what's the matter with me. I've been awake all night. My face feels like a balloon, and the pain is driving me mad! So, have you got anymore damn fool questions?" and Geller groaned and resumed his perambulations. He was certainly very pale, and his face was visibly swollen on one side.

"Well there is no bloody point on walking up and down, is there? That's not going to do much good. The thing to do is to have the tooth looked at, and quick, and if necessary you'll have to have it out!" Herbert, as ever, was being reasonable.

"I'm not going to no bloody dentist," Geller moaned again.

"I saw a camp hospital yesterday, somewhere down by the main gate," Herbert said."I don't know anything about it, or what they've got inside it, but we could go down and see if they can do anything for you. Blimey! Even if they can only give you a couple of pills, I think it'd be better than walking up and down moaning and groaning, with a bloody toothache."

"It's not your bloody toothache," snapped Geller. "It's me that's got the toothache. It's my tooth, and it's me that'll have to have the thing taken out, I suppose." "Oh! Please yourself. It's us that will have to listen to you groaning all the time. Come on, let's have a walk down there, and see if they can do anything for you. I'll come with you, if you like. If you don't like the look of things when we get there, we can always come back."

Geller allowed himself to be persuaded, and they walked together in the direction where Herbert thought he had seen the Red Cross. He was right! It was there, in a shed by the main gate, with the word 'Medico' on the door. "Right," Herbert said, with purpose in his tone.

"Now we've got here, we might as well have a look. I'll ask for something for a headache, and you can look around. If you don't think much of it, we'll just go back to the hut. Ready?" Geller nodded, and they went inside.

A little fat German with a round red face, with a Red Cross armband, came bustling up to them, and asked what he could do for them.

"I've got a splitting headache," said Herbert, "can you give me something for it?" Away went the little chap, almost running in his desire to prove himself useful, to return within a couple of seconds with a couple of tablets in the palm of his hands, and these he handed to Herbert. They looked remarkably like aspirin. Geller, with his face afire, let out a subdued groan, and the little orderly, with ill-concealed delight, looked at his face. "Aha," he said to Herbert. "Your friend need the dentist?"

"Yes," said Herbert.

"No!" groaned Geller.

"Yes! Yes!" fussed the orderly. "Of course! You go in there and wait, he will be there in a few minutes," and he ushered the unwilling Geller through the door into the inner room.

"Don't worry," Herbert patted Geller's suffering shoulder.

"It won't take long. I'll wait for you outside." And he left the building, as Geller with a look of abject terror on his swollen face, followed the bustling orderly into the inner sanctum.

Herbert waited outside, leaning on the corner of the hut, whistling 'Lili Marlene' and trying to remember all the dirty words, until Geller reappeared some twenty minutes later. He was holding his head with both hands, and moaning, "Bloody butcher! Mein Gott, what a butcher! Oh! My head. It's coming off…" and so on.

"Alright then, mate?" Herbert asked with the air of a man who is determined to remain cheerful at all costs.

"Alright? Alright?" Geller's voice rose. "What I've been through you will never know. That man! I can't believe it! He pulled two and drilled three! He works like a conveyor belt, with the sensitivity of a tank!"

He leaned against the hut, and wiped a spot of blood from the corner of his mouth.

"Well, you don't look too bad. The swelling has gone down a bit already."

"You should see the drill he is using," said Geller, in a tone of awe and wonder. "I've never seen anything like it. I think it must have been contrived by that chap – what's his name? Robinson. Heath Robinson. It must be homemade! Surely, British dentistry has progressed beyond that?"

He paused, and then said, "Look! There is a chair, see?" and he made chair shaped circles with his hands, so Herbert could not possibly be under any misapprehension. "And attached to the chair is a sort of bicycle attachment. With pedals! Honestly! With pedals! I ask you?"

And here he did a little groaning for effect.

"Do you know what you have to do? You have to sit in his bloody chair, and you, yes you, have to pedal the drill! Pedal the drill, with your mouth open, and full of his fist. You can't breathe, and the faster he wants to drill, the faster he shouts at you to pedal. You are already in pain. You work up a fine sweat with the exertion of pedalling, and you gasp for breath, with your mouth wide open. Oh my God."

They were almost at Hut 28, and Geller sank down to the steps. "My God, Herbert," he said with feeling. "Never again! No matter what happens. Never again. Every bloody tooth in my head can ache at once, and can fall out and drop on the floor for all I care. My bloody head can fall off. But never again will I go back there."

He paused, and looked at Herbert in a tragi-comic face, making sure that he had understood. "Now," he said. "Help me back to my bed if you will, and just allow me to die quietly and without any further fuss, and if you're still looking for a way to be helpful, find a piece of paper and write a verse for my grave stone." A very faint thin scream issued forth the direction of the dental hut. Herbert and Geller looked at each other.

"Poor sod," they said in unison, and Herbert put Geller to bed.

Karl Krohn, from Hut 16, had struck one of those passing prison friendships with someone in Hut 28, and on one of his frequent visits, he told them about the project upon which he was working, and which occupied a great deal of his waking thought. He was trying to produce an acceptable cigarette by experimenting with all the 'throw-away' rubbish and garbage lying around the camp.

It was a well-known fact that the prisoners who had undergone even meagre medical training in the German army always somehow managed to get a ready supply of good cigarettes. Karl gave much thought to this phenomenon, and made judicious enquires, which he reported faithfully back to Hut 28. Apparently, he learned, about once a month, the Red Cross from Switzerland send parcels to the POW camps in England. The 'medics' received these parcels first, being Red Cross and all that, and thus had first pick of the goods they contained. Then the Lagerführer and his little band of merry men had their share, and, being careful, they naturally kept a little aside for a rainy day. Like when no parcels arrived, or arrived late and if there was any at all left by then, the rest of the prisoners might, if they were very lucky, get a bit of it.

Karl greatly bemoaned the fact that he was not a 'medic', and had never volunteered for this line of duty. But it was too late to do anything about it now. Necessity is undoubtedly the mother of invention, and he brought the full power of his Teutonic brain to bear upon the problem.

He lay in his bunk, legs crossed and hands behind his head, gasping for a smoke, and determined to get one somehow. In fact, better still, to get a supply. "I wonder," he mused, "what happens to all the tea leaves from the cook-house? They must use a hell of a lot of tea, and they must have to put the leaves somewhere."

Galvanised into action, he decided to reconnoître. He wandered slowly over towards the cook-house, playing it cool so as to not arouse anyone's suspicions, and he leaned against the corner of the hut, hands in pockets, staring vacantly in space, and whistling under his breath. He watched the back door closely. Hung inside were about eight dustbins, and clouds of steam issued forth from the half-opened back window. The door opened, one of the cooks emerged, heading towards the bins, with a bucket of waste. Karl strolled towards him.

"Here mate," he said, "what happened to the tea leaves after you have brewed up for the camp?"

The cook looked puzzled. "Tea leaves? What leaves?"

"The leaves you pour the boiling water on to," Karl explained with the air of one speaking to an infant. "Oh! You mean the pie-warm turd we serve up to you lot. Well, there's a few leaves in there sometimes, but mostly it's dust or tea powder. Why?"

"Just wondering," Karl said. "Just an idea I had that's all."

"Well," the cook went on, "whatever is left after the brew goes into the bins with the rest of the muck." He paused and tipped the bucket he was carrying into the bin. "It's all in there, if you want it…" and he grinned.

Karl looked into the bin. It was unspeakably repulsive, and he thought he saw maggots. He couldn't really bring himself to rake through the contents just to get some used tea leaves. There must be another way. Brewed or unbrewed didn't really matter.

As it happened, Karl was on the meal rota for his hut that same evening, and with his hut-mate he made his way to the same canteen to collect the evening rations. Tea, bread and jam as usual. Karl waited patiently in the queue, and shuffled slowly forward when, quite unexpectedly, out of the corner of his eye he spotted a cardboard box, full of tea. It was standing on a table just on the inner door of the cookhouse. The line of waiting men moved slowly forward, and as quick as a flash, and with no time to think,

64

Karl darted over to the box, grabbed a packet of tea, and thrust it inside his shirt. One of the cocks turned around, and looked at him hard, but if he spotted a squarish bulge under Karl's armpit, he said nothing.

"God that was a close thing." Karl felt himself begin to sweat a little. He and his mate collected their rations, and returned to their hut.

Karl was jubilant! 'So far so good,' he told himself as he wolfed down his share of bread and jam. 'Now all I need is a bit of paper, and I've got it!'

A bit of paper was not easy to come by. In fact, there seemed to be a total dearth of paper all around the camp. Even the bog paper was almost always missing, and in any case, was 'medicated'. At least that's what it said on it. Karl wandered all around the camp, until at length he spotted a small square hanging drunkenly from a single inadequate drawing pin, on the notice board. At some time, in the past, it had probably held some vital piece of information, written in ink, but little traces of this now remained. Karl felt it. It was a bit thick perhaps, but needs must when the devil drives, so he tore it free, folded it and put it in his pocket.

Back at the hut he carefully measured it, and tore it into suitable sized rectangular strips. One of these he filled with the loose tea he pinched from the canteen, and rolled it up. He had no glue to fix it, so he licked it well, and twisted both ends.

This remarkable operation was watched with absorbed curiosity by the other inmates of the hut. Those who were heavy and habitual smokers, hopeful. The others stood with a fairly detached interest.

All eyes focussed on Karl as he struck a match on the wall, and lit the twisted end of the misshapen cigarette hanging from the corner of his mouth. He inhaled deeply. Clouds of blue smoke filled the air around his bunk, and the smell was both indefinable and unbelievable. Suddenly, he was overcome with a fit of coughing. He hacked and retched, his eyes streamed, and he seemed likely to choke. Well-meaning mates thumped him on the back in an effort to be helpful.

"I think I must have made it a bit too strong," he was heard to say, between paroxysm.

"My God, Karl," they all said, as they stood around him. "What the hell have you got rolled up in there?"

"It's a new breakthrough," Karl choked with difficulty. "English tea fags."

"Well it stinks like a cross between old socks and cheesy feet so get the bloody things out of here."

"If we have to sleep in here with that stink, we could suffocate. We might even wake up dead."

Karl was too glad to go outside. In fact, he was halfway out of the door, and running, before the last speaker had finished. Suddenly, he felt rather sick.

Early the next morning, the camp witnessed him rushing agitatedly to and fro, backwards and forwards, between the hut and the latrine block until, as someone said, there must be a well-defined groove along the route he took. Actually, he spent the greater part of the day inside the latrine block. English tea fags had given him the 'runs' good and proper.

"I don't think I've got it quite yet," he kept saying in answer to enquires. "I'm making them too strong."

He took out his handkerchief and mopped his sallow face.

"I think I shall have a go at mixing something else with it. I can't keep going on like this… it's playing havoc with my guts...!"

Herbert and Erwin were sitting on the steps of the hut, playing in a desultory fashion, a game they had invented. It was a variation of the old Five-Stones, playing with round flattish pebbles, collected from the very edge of the compound, and with number inked on them. Erwin, as usual, was winning.

At the far end of the camp, a working party of Tommies seemed to be erecting an eight-foot-high barbed wire fence, right through the exact middle of the existing compound, splitting the camp in two halves. "What do you think they are doing?" Erwin was curious. "Perhaps they think we've got too much room, and are cutting us down."

"Who knows? Could be anything…"

They watched as the working party completed the job, apparently to everyone's satisfaction, and then disappeared. Almost immediately: "Roll-call! Roll-call!"

"Gott on Himmel! Already?" Erwin was on his feet. "We only had a bloody roll-call half an hour ago. Surely they don't think we've had time to dig a tunnel since then…?"

The camp was assembled, and standing to attention. Through an interpreter, the prisoners were informed that they were to be politically graded. The camp would be divided into two separate compounds – hence the fence – and in future it would be known as Camp A and Camp B. Erwin dug Herbert in the ribs.

"I suppose they mean that if you've got a crooked face, they class you as a political danger," he grinned. Herbert took a much more serious view. He felt distinctly uncomfortable. "Don't be so bloody daft," he said. "This lot aren't stupid! They must have some reason for doing this, and whatever it is, I don't like it. It'll come back on us in the long run, and I don't like it at all…"

At length it was made clear to them, just as Herbert has supposed. They were told in no uncertain terms, that if they were ready to accept total defeat, change their political views, they would be well taken care of, be well fed and looked after, and be transferred to Camp B. At this, a loud laugh rang through the assembled prisoners.

"The bloody cheek of it! The war's still on, isn't it? We are not defeated… yet!" Who the hell was going to 'turncoat' at this stage?

But although they laughed, it upset everybody. There was an uneasy atmosphere, and the prisoners talked of little else for the rest of the day, turning all aspects over and over in their minds. This was something that each person was going to decide for himself.

Small groups collected together, and factions began to form. In a couple of days, it was quite easy to pick them all out. There were the obvious Nazi's, the half-Nazi's, and the strong left-wingers. And, of course the 'don't-knows' and quite a few of the 'don't-much-cares'. Everyone was trying to convert all the others to his own way of thinking, and heated arguments lasting all night disturbed them all, so that some feverish hut swapping took place. Tension mounted, and anger ran very high, sometimes even exploding into violence in the form of a punch-up. A few swollen faces and black eyes were seen around the camp.

Herbert didn't join in any of the established groups. He tried the think the whole thing over coherently, quietly be himself, but could come to no real decision. Certainly not an honest one. He couldn't change all his political views and briefs as if they had never existed.

He had, like many of the others shouting their mouths off around the place, believed in the Führer and the Third Reich. He never had any doubts. The man was undoubtedly a genius, a great leader, and he had promised to make Germany a great power in the world again. If force had to be used as a last resort, then they would use it, they were not afraid. This is what the Führer had told the German people, and they, and Herbert had believed it implicitly.

He remembered his days in the Hitler Youth with some pride. He even had been privileged to march in a rally which had been honoured by the presence of the Führer. How proud they all had been, how grateful. What a sense of patriotism and glory he had kindled within them all. Young and impressionable, they had stood at attention, and listened to him, their ideal, their inspiration.

He thought of all this now, as the arguments raged around him. What had happened to the dismembered glory? Where had it all gone wrong? At what point did it start to crumble? All the ideals, the ivory towers, the dreams, all in ruins. Was it all in ruins? Could Germany, his beloved land, ever rise again out of this holocaust? He, Herbert, was a simple straight-forward man, and he didn't know.

It was all too complex for a simple man to understand, he thought, but then, neither could a simple man just casually drop all the things he had formerly believed in, and pretend that they no longer existed. Especially just because a British soldier, who was his hated enemy, told him that it would be much better for him to do so.

Herbert might change his ideas slowly, over a period of time. Most people adapt to circumstances, and Herbert was particularly good at this. But not at once, immediately, without notice, without further thought. This was not Herbert's nature.

He did not care too much about what other people thought of him, but he did care about what he thought of himself. He had to go on living with himself, indefinitely, as he put it. So, he joined in no arguments, united with no groups, and kept quiet.

Hut 38 rapidly turned itself into the headquarters of the Party for the Third Reich. Aguste Ackerman, a sergeant from the paratroopers, and a man of ideas, was elected head of operations. His feelings were running very high, and he left no one in any doubt at all about where he stood. He addressed his 'party' at every available opportunity. "Let's show the Tommies all is not lost," he would roar. A mild cheer would be raised at this, and Ackerman raised his hands above his head in silence, with the air and manner of a Hollywood star after greeting his fans. "Just because we are held in captivity, that is not to say that we cannot continue to carry out the Führer's wishes. Let us remember them, and give these British something to think about. We well organise rallies, demonstrations, meetings, even a torchlight procession."

At this latter suggestion, his eyes glowed with patriotic fervour, and Herbert wondered if Ackerman had ever taken part in one of the famous Hitler Youth Rallies.

Hut 38 was a hive of activity. Anyone they were not sure of was dragged in and bombarded with questions. If their answers were not considered satisfactory, they attempted to 'brainwash' them, for Hut 38 was in no doubt. They were still, and would ever remain, German soldiers. United is what they considered to be their just cause, they worked desperately to unite their fellow soldiers.

Aguste Ackerman began to look, and to talk like Hitler himself, and strutted around the compound like, as Herbert thought silently, a turkey cock on a midden. With a great difficulty, and a few false starts, a can of cooking oil was stolen from the cookhouse, together with a few sacks. These were torn into strips, wound round bits of wood, and thoroughly soaked in oil. For these were to be the torches.

Ackerman was ecstatic.

"Tonight, we shall have our torchlight procession. After 'lights-out', of course. That will give them something to think about. They will not split this camp into half. They will see that we are united, that we are German soldiers."

Word went around that anyone wishing to take part should report to Hut 38, where they would receive full instructions. 'What the hell are they having a torchlight procession for?' Herbert wanted to know, when word was passed to him on the camp grapevine.

"Search me," his informant was non-committal. "I think the Nazi's are on the parade again...!"

Herbert too was non-committal. "Well, it should break the monotony at least," he said. The other chap looked hard at him.

"Maybe," he said, "But I'm afraid it might break more than that!"

Lights out was at ten o'clock and the camp was in total darkness, except for the main gate which was kept brilliantly lit at all times. Herbert, and a few mates, stood by the door of their hut, mostly out of idle curiosity, just to see what, if anything was going to happen. They were not sure just how far Ackerman and his gang would go with this idea.

Suddenly, by arrangement, a veritable cacophony of clattering and banging came from the direction of Hut 38. It literally split the silence of the night for two or three minutes, and then all was quiet again. The hut door flew open, and the first few torches appeared, marching in the inevitable files of three, they made their way towards the centre of the compound, and they were singing at the top of their voices the German national anthem, 'Deutschland' and 'Die Fahne Hoch.'

It was quite a brave sight really, Herbert thought, almost with regret. The shadowy figures, their faces illuminated but faintly by the glow of their cooking oil torches, heads up and shoulders back, their boots hitting the tarmacadam compound in unison, and their voices – not good voices, but strong – belting out the words of the songs they had sung and lived for all these years.

The torches gave good light, but they smoked like hell, and it hung over the whole compound like a pall. There must have been about fifty prisoners in the procession, Herbert decided, attempting to do a rough count of the bobbing lights. Then, just as suddenly as it started, it stopped. Torches were simultaneously stamped out. The camp was once again in total darkness, and a few seconds silence, the whole parade scattered in several directions, back to their sleeping quarters.

A short couple of moments later, the loud speaker system was galvanised into strident action. "Roll-call!" Roll-call!" and lights blazed all over the camp.

"Christ! That buggered it," Herbert said wearily to Geller.

"Now we're all getting clobbered for this little episode!" It was not far short of midnight, and grumbling and cussing, the entire camp stood to attention.

Half an hour passed, and nothing happened. Then the Tommies arrived in numbers, and held what appeared to be a heated consultation with Major Kohler, the

71

Lagerführer. Herbert could see him nodding his head and clicking his heels like a wound-up tin toy. Then apparently on the instruction of the Tommies, he addressed the shivering prisoners.

"This special roll-call has been ordered by the English commandant. It has been brought to his attention that a certain group of men are set upon the disruption of the smooth running of this camp. A stupid and pointless performance. The torchlight procession has given grave cause for concern. The commandant is exceedingly upset and angry about the whole affair, and those of you who are responsible must be punished. I am asking you, as your Lagerführer, to step forward and own up! Who is responsible for this ridiculous escapade?"

A ripple of ribald laughter greeted this, and the ranks of the assembled prisoners shuffled. In this at least they were wholly united. Nobody had organised anything, and nobody had taken part in anything. The strutting pompous little figure of Kohler could run around in ever decreasing circles until… but he would get nothing out of this lot. They all knew what he wanted alright. To suck up to this British and look after number one. And they were not about to help him.

Nobody spoke or moved. Minutes ticked by. Kohler was beginning to look a bit silly, standing there in front of the ranks of his own men, all silently watching him, and delighting in his discomfiture. He marched up and down a bit and clasped and unclasped his hands behind his back. But still nobody spoke. He had another whispered conversation with the British officer, and then he came forward, and addressed them again.

"If those responsible do not come forward, the entire camp will suffer. I have been assured that you will remain all night if need be."

'Looks as if we are going to be here for a long time,' Herbert thought, trying to shift his weight from one foot to the other, and feeling pins and needles in his right calf. He knew these fanatical types. They never gave in, not even when it was quite obviously hopeless to hold out.

Another hour went by, and still nobody had moved or spoken. 'God, why don't they bloody well own up and we can all get some sleep,' groaned the little man inside Herbert's head. A few prisoners were dozing on their feet, their eyes fixed open, and others were surreptitiously shuffling, or attempting to rub their hands on the sides of their legs. It was getting cold, and as the night ground slowly on, it got colder still, and the air was penetratingly damp. The guards patrolled along the back and crossed at the front. A heavy and cumbersome silence lay over all.

At four o'clock in the morning, came just one order 'Dismiss' and with some difficulty the prisoners limped stiffly back to their huts and into their bunks. "I doubt if we've heard the last of this night's work," Herbert muttered below his breath, as he clambered into his top bunk, and dragged the blanket over his head. "You're damn right, mate," came in low key from the direction of Geller's bunk. "You're too damn right…"

Hut 39 had among its inmates some well-established snoopers. They drifted quietly about the camp, unobtrusive, listening here, and passing slowly by there. Whatever information they had happened to glean was passed on to wherever it would do the most good, purely for personal and material gain, usually via Major Kohler and his cohorts. There was a tall, thin lugubrious looking chap who shuffled about with his shoulders hunched as if permanently cold, and a little round chap with him with a snub nose and bright ginger hair. They were always to be seen walking around together, and it became obvious to everyone what they were up to. They looked shifty, and furtive. They could not even act up very well, for their air of required nonchalance was so transparent, it was pathetic.

They would drift up to a group of men deep in conversation, and in seconds the group would split up and go its separate ways. They were to be found just around every corner, just below every window. Nobody wanted to know them, nobody would talk to them, and their presence put an immediate stop to all conversation, however innocent the talk was. They became the camp pariahs to be avoided at all costs.

About eleven o'clock one morning, just a short time after the episode of the torchlight procession, four guards and an officer were seen to enter the camp, accompanied by the Lagerführer and they made their way, the cynosure of all eyes, to Hut 38. All idle activity stopped, and the prisoners waited to see what was going to happen, for it was obvious something was afoot.

Then, Aguste Ackerman appeared, flanked by the guards, front and rear, and was marched to the main gates and outside. As he was about to be ushered through the main gate, Ackerman turned, realising that all his hut-mates followed in a ragged sort of procession. He clicked his heels with enviable military precision, gave the Nazi salute – and a wide grin, and wads peremptorily marched off.

A quavering cheer broke out, but everyone present immediately realised what happened.

"Someone has grassed to the British," said Willi Springer, who was a mate of Ackerman's, and slept in the bunk below him.

"By God! The little toad! If I find out who did this… If I catch the bastard…"

Herbert found it rather hard to understand all the steam that had been generated on both sides by the entire episode. Alright, so it had been a kind of 'thumb to the nose' gesture. But so what? They were all still prisoners, locked in and guarded all day and night. They could not really do anything. All they had really done was affront the British by virtually putting up two fingers, and temporarily disrupt the smooth running of the camp, which was all that seemed to concern Kohler anyway.

They had been punished, like naughty schoolboys, by being made to stand outside in the cold for most of the night. So what? They had time! Time was the only thing that they did not have in quantity, and in retrospect, the affair seemed childish.

Herbert did not say it out loud, but his private opinion was that if the British had ignored the torchlight procession, pretended that they had never seen it, even regarded with tolerant amusement, then Ackerman would have been made to look silly instead of being turned into some kind of 'Prisoner's Hero' at the present.

Later, that day, the news got around that Ackerman was in solitary confinement for twenty-one days for being the ringleader in the torchlight business. 'Poor Sod!' said Herbert, with feeling, and promptly forgot all about it.

But Willi Springer did not. He was now more determined than ever to find the 'traitor' as he kept referring to it. He organised his own group, filled them with spurious fervour, and set them to work. It didn't take long. A word here, a hint there and a glance in the right direction. It was pretty obvious anyway that it must be one of the two snoopers from Hut 39, and Willi now knew which one.

One evening, after roll-call, Willi and two of his hut-mates strolled casually around the compound. At least they hoped for it to look casual, because they were really looking for the 'traitor'. Ginger was on his way back from the lavatory. Quite chirpy he was. His hair seemed redder than ever, and the rimless glasses he used for reading were precariously perched on the bright of his snub nose. A dog-eared copy of a paperback Western was clutched in his hand and bore mute tribute to his earnest desire to improve his knowledge of the English language! Willi lengthened his stride and caught up with him. "Ah Ginger," said Willi, with a disarming smile. "I was wondering where you had got to. I want a word with you."

"What about?" Ginger said, a glazed look coming over his face, as Willi took him companionably by the arm, and propelled him towards the rear of the huts.

"You know! Don't play games with me," Willi's voice changed once they were out of sight of the rest of the camp.

"Auguste is in solitary for three weeks, and you're the one that put him there. You grassed."

"Not me, not me! You got the wrong chap, honest," Ginger's voice was a squeak, and he was plainly terrified. He put both of his hands out in front of his body as if to ward off some threat.

"Never. I never grassed on anyone."

"You grassed. You pig!" Willi's voice was low and venomous.

"You call yourself a German, and yet you betray your mates to the Tommies. You're a rotten traitor, a liar and a coward!" Willi seemed to tower over the little fat man, who was wilting visibly beneath this barrage and the hatred in Willi's eyes.

"You leave me alone," he squeaked again. "Leave me alone or I'll report you to the Lagerführer."

"Yeah, I should. Why don't you?" And Willi picked the little man up by the back of his collar until his feet swung free from the ground and slapped him a couple of times around the face so that his head jerked from one side, and then the other. Then he let him drop on the ground.

"You rat," he said contemptuously.

At this, Ginger seemed to gather some last vestige of his enfeebled courage, "Anyway. Why should the whole camp suffer for your pointless and stupid demonstration? You all should have owned up and then the rest of us would not have been punished."

This speech was enough to convince Willi that this was indeed the right man. That was all he wanted to know. His lips twisted, and he strode away leaving Ginger shaking at the back of the hut.

"You're not letting him off that easily, Willi?" His mates were a little incredulous.

"Don't worry," Willi said. "I have my own plan. I know exactly what to do with a little turd like that…"

Willi certainly had a plan, and he had worked it all out to the finest detail. It would serve the bloody creep right!

It was after midnight, and the camp had settled down. All was quiet and dark, and the only movement was that of the occasional prisoner walking across the compound to the latrine block. Willi and his two partners made their way to Hut 39, keeping close within the shadow of the hut walls, and moving without sound. Willi opened the door without so much as a squeak, and the three of them went in. They knew which one was Ginger's bed and headed towards it. Willi's steely fingers fastened around his mouth, cutting him off in mid-snore. Quickly and silently, the fat man was enveloped in a blanket and carried out of the hut. He struggled violently and in terror, but to no avail. Willi's fingers were like a vice. No one spoke.

The three of them carried him, a mere blanket-wrapped bundle, passed the last few huts, and threw him on the ground, with Willi on top of him to keep him still. His hand was still over Ginger's mouth, and the little man was beginning to foam and his eyes protrude.

"If you make one sound, I'll strangle you right now," Willi hissed, and made sure that Ginger understood by giving his snub nose a painful twist with each syllable. In front of them was the camp cesspit! A large underground chamber which frequently exuded a miasma which defied explanation. Its lid was a flat concrete slab.

One of Willi's mates produced a length of rope from his inside pocket and working swiftly as if they were used to this, they gagged and bound Ginger securely with the blanket over his head. They roped him tightly around his flabby belly.

"Right," Willi said, when he was sure that Ginger could hear him, but make no noise. "Now you understand. You dropped us in it, you miserable little swine. So... we return the compliment, and we drop you in it..."

The heavy lid was dragged aside from the cesspit, and the eerie 'gloppy' sound of turgid sewage could be heard. Ginger heard it and found new strength. He struggled frantically inside the grey blanket, but even in terror, he could not free himself, or even loosen the bonds. He tried to scream, but no sound emerged.

With the three of them holding the rope, slowly and with a sense of justice, almost a ritual, they lowered the package that was Ginger into the evil smelling morass.

"Leave him there for a few hours," Willi said, and they made the end of the rope fast. "Perhaps this will teach him what happens to a soldier who grasses on their mates..." And the three of them returned to Hut 38, as quietly as they had come.

At about four o'clock in the morning, Willi and the two mates, awakened from their slumber and feeling refreshed, dressed swiftly and returned to the scene of retribution. In the greyish light of the half-dawn, they removed the lid of the cesspit, and hauled Ginger back into the world of the living. He was stiff as a board, and frozen almost into a solid lump. The stench that arose from the grey flannel blanket was thick, almost tangible, and being loath to touch any part of the bundle, they dragged it by the rope, and moved it with their feet, right back down the length of the camp, passed the still silent huts, and left it outside the washroom. It had been sufficiently loosened to allow Ginger to escape as best as he might.

Ginger never got himself into any more trouble after this rough justice. He was no more seen to be lurking in the corners or listening beneath windows. If anyone approached him at all he scurried in the opposite direction. He was, as you might say, completely cured.

Camp B was not ready for occupation. Despite all the efforts of the inmates of Hut 38 to keep the prisoners united, the split had been achieved. Two lines of prisoners left for one half of the camp and moved to the other side of the barbed wire fence. For them, to traverse the two lines of prisoners was rather like a game of running the gauntlet, established by the North American Indians. They were heckled, reviled, spat upon and called all the names that the German forces could lay tongue to. They were 'traitors', 'cowards' 'Tommies bum-boys' and worse. But they were marched out, and the camp was thus successfully split into two fractions. The onlooker saw most of the game, and Herbert watched this one from a safe distance.

Life in Camp A went on as usual, but the departure had naturally left gaps. There was an undercurrent of anger, a sense of betrayal. There was bitterness and a hardening, but like most wounds, after a while the skin began to heal across the raw surface.

It would not have been so bad if the occupants remaining did not have such a good view of the better life of Camp B, but as they strolled aimlessly about, with endless time on their hands, and the intolerable burden of complete boredom, they could see all kinds of things being organised for the prisoners in the other half of the camp. Some sports equipment was made available, and games were organised.

But the thing that really hurt Herbert most of all was when he saw some musical instruments being delivered 'over the wire' and later, heard them being played, and the sound of singing which carried on sometimes until after lights out.

Herbert had never been much a man for games, and sports, but how he loved music, and how he missed it. His captivity would have been just that little bit easier, and he felt that he could have coped just that little bit better, if only he was able to listen, or even make some music. Even a mouth organ would have been enough. He remembered the days of the jazz band, and how he and Fritz had played for the people on the river at home.

Morale in Camp A began to suffer, and there was no doubt that the Tommies had won this battle. Things were not improved when the rations grew less and less each day. The pea or bean soup which was the regular lunch was getting more and more watery. Frequently it was possible to see the bottom of the can, there was so little substance in the mixture.

Hunger played havoc with Herbert! He realised that he was getting almost light-headed, and he could think of little else but food. There must be some way of improving their diet, if only he could work something out. Around one of the huts – in fact, around most of the huts – there were patches of stinging nettles. He remembered his Aunt Elsa, good countrywoman that she was, saying that young turkeys would do well on a good boiling of nettles. They were very good for them, she had said, and they contained a lot of iron. Even as a girl, she had told him, she had prepared a boiling of young nettle tops in the spring, and they were as good a cabbage, when young. Perhaps this was the answer, and perhaps their meagre diet was deficient in iron. It was certainly deficient in quantity, he thought.

Herbert was a great one for self-help, so he picked the young green tops of the nettles, chopped them as small as he could, and it was not long before the other prisoners followed suit. In a couple of weeks, there was not a single nettle to be found on the entire camp. They had all been eaten. So popular it was, that as soon a plant popped its head above the ground, two prisoners were standing there waiting it pick it.

In the meantime, Camp B were really living well. It appeared as they were enjoying one long party. Camp A could see loaves of bread being passed out, and even offered them at the wire. But Camp A didn't want to know. They had some pride left, so they threw the bread back, and suffered from hunger. They were not going to be 'bought' by a pitiful loaf of bread, even though it was white. They felt that having made a stand thus far, they must continue with it, and they considered that Camp B had 'sold out' to the enemy.

One morning, after the usual roll-call, the first two columns of one hundred prisoners were asked to remain standing to attention, and the remainder were dismissed. 'Mein Gott! What now?' Herbert's thoughts chased each other round and around inside his head.

"You will leave this camp in one hours' time, so collect your belongings and assemble back here at nine o'clock," said one of Kohler's merry men.

Relieved or disappointed, the prisoners dispersed. "On the bloody move again," Herbert muttered. "Where to now? Why and what for?" It might be better. On the other hand, he supposed it could be a damn sight worse. A choice between cholera and the plague, but as usual, he would do as he was told. Anyway, he reflected, the nettles might still be growing wherever it was they were going. They were useful, and he had developed quite a taste for them.

One hundred Prisoners of War assembled by the main gate of Camp 17 and set off under heavy guard for an unknown (to them) destination. The sky had clouded over, and a light drizzle was falling. "Can't be too bad, wherever we are going." Herbert was determined to be optimistic. "There's one thing about it," he said to the chap marching alongside. "We're more of England this way then those left behind. Even if it is bloody well raining again…"

He turned around for a last look at the fast disappearing Camp 17, where he had left his mate, Erwin, and resolutely turned his face and his thoughts – forward.

Chapter V:

Camp 29 (Cambridgeshire)

By mid-afternoon, the rain had stopped, and a watery sun shone fitfully on the autumn tinted leaves, as Herbert and ninety-nine others arrived at their new camp. They stood, stamping their booted feet against the seasonal nip of the air, as the guard counted them. The main gate swung open and crashed behind them with the ringing finality. In front of them the usual barbed wire fencing. It seemed at the time as if the whole wide world was totally enmeshed in barbed wires, rolls and rolls of the stuff, from which it was frantically, endeavouring to break free. Tired, thirsty and heavy eyed from the journey, they waited.

This camp was already teeming with German POWs, strolling around the compound, bustling about, and Herbert looked at them with dawning astonishment. They all wore chocolate coloured uniforms, and had brightly coloured squares and circles sewn on their tunics and trousers. 'My God!' he thought, silently. 'This is the German army? We have come to this? They look like a bunch of comics.'

But then he looked again, he realised that overall, they looked a damn cheerful bunch of comics. They were alert, smiling. They looked tidy and they did not seem to have lost their personal dignity, as had so many others. They waved and greeted each other, and strode purposefully about the place as if they really had something to do, something that was important to them, and not just contrived to help to pass the time hanging around.

The Lagerführer approached. "You look to me like a lot of tired soldiers," he said, kindly but briskly.

"The first thing to do is to get you billeted, and then we will see if we can get you some food. You all look as if you could do with a square meal."

Herbert reflected that this was probably the most sensible thing he had heard anyone say in weeks. He always felt much better about everything after he had eaten, and he only wished he could eat more often.

He was put in Hut No.7, right at the back, near a window. The familiar double tiered bunks were not as high as in the last camp. The chap seated on the lower bunk grinned at Herbert cheerfully and extended his hand. "Alfred Jackel," he said.

He was rather short and of stocky build, with the broad shoulders and thick upper arms that generally go with manual work. The hand that he held out to Herbert was square with spatulate fingers, and the nails were clipped right down. His face was round and shiny, surmounted by a veritable bush of curly blonde hair which, despite repeated applications of water to make it stick down, sprang out all around his head.

"Our new hotel," he said, "and they have promised us some food. It looks good, doesn't it?"

Herbert was cautious. "Well, it seems better than my last one. There seems to be quite a jolly atmosphere around the place. I hope they let us stay put for a while for a bit, so we can sort of 'recharge our batteries', if you know what I mean. I got damn fed up with the last 'hotel', and all the political intrigue, and yammering."

They sat on Alfred's bunk and exchanged a few personal details. It soon became obvious that Alfred was a bit of a comic himself. He had a dry way of commenting on life that soon set Herbert smiling. He found that he liked him, and thought it would be easy to get on alright with Alfred. There were no undertones here. Alfred's life was, in effect, an open book. He was frank, humorous, and a born optimist, and just a bit of a rascal.

It was not for Alfred, the inner turmoil of the rights and wrongs of the Third Reich; he just went on living his life along fairly straight lines, winning a bit here, losing a bit there. Any obstacles that lay across his path he surmounted with the best will and dignity he could muster. He was a man after Herbert's own heart! A bugle sounded outside. "What the hell...?" Alfred leapt to his feet.

One chap stuck his head outside the hut to investigate and, pulling it back again, reported to the rest that it seemed to be yet another roll-call. The arrangement at Camp 29 differed only in that they were told to line up in fives instead of threes. The whole camp stood to attention and the Tommies entered by the main gate, rifles shouldered. The Lagerführer saluted smartly, and the count began. Five, ten, fifteen, twenty... they made marks upon their pads, then added it all up, and compared notes. Of the numbers tallied, they obviously concluded that everyone was present and accounted for.

A further salute from the Lagerführer, and the Tommies departed whilst the prisoners returned to their huts. The next thing was the eagerly awaited promised food, and there again the system differed only slightly. In the centre of the camp was a big barrack building which contained a dining hall and the camp kitchen. Meals were served here in two sittings, and of the six hundred or so prisoners, half ate at six p.m. and the other half three quarters of an hour later. It took the new arrivals no time at all to get the hang of the dining arrangements, and Herbert and Alfred, lucky once again, came within the first batch. Queuing in single file, they shuffled along slowly until they came to a pile of tin plates. Everyone grabbed one, then shuffled a little further along until they stood in front of the cooks. Holding out the tin plate, it was filled full of potatoes, cabbage, a little meat and gravy, and a chunk of white bread.

Herbert's eyes widened as he saw his plate filled to capacity, and the smell of the steam arising from the hot food set his saliva glands working overtime. True, it was mostly vegetables, but he hadn't seen food like this, nor in such quantities, for a very long time. He'd thought about it! Colourful pictures of steaming food flickered across his brain in the still of the night, as he lay half-awake, half-asleep. The little man inside his head seemed to delight in pointing out culinary pleasures to Herbert, that he could not hope to have, and these pictures increased the pangs of hunger rumbling around his belly.

Well, here was food, and for the first time since his capture, Herbert felt that the amount he had been given might just be enough to assuage his immediate hunger. He sat down with Alfred, and silently they enjoyed their first meal in Camp 29. To them, the taste of plain, ill-cooked food was an unmitigated delight. An offering of nectar and ambrosia, whatever it is, could hardly have been more gratefully received. They concentrated hard upon the full plates in front of them, trying with some difficulty to force themselves to eat slowly, and neither spoke until the last crumb of bread had successfully chased the last vestige of gravy in their gullets. Alfred leaned back and sucked his teeth to remove the last morsels. Then he said, "Well! If they keep serving food like this, I think I'll stay until the end of the war…" and he grinned at Herbert.

Back in the hut, they found one of the officials waiting for them. The Lagerführer wanted to see all the new arrivals, and asked that they attend the dining hall at eight o'clock, and not be late!

"I rather like the dining hall," Herbert said, as he lay replete on his bunk. "I wonder where they leave the leftovers…"

"You can't still be hungry?"

"I've got a lot to make up, you know," Herbert indignantly justified himself.

Eight o'clock saw them all assembled, as requested, and eventually the Lagerführer arrived, accompanied by two of his officers, with an armful of papers. The chatter stopped, and all eyes were riveted upon him.

"My name is Lt. Schroder," he began. "I am your chief in Camp 29. First, let me tell you a bit about this place. We, that is some of us, have been here for nine months, and at this moment we enjoy quite a reasonable existence, even though we are captive. Our relations with the English are… acceptable, and we make the most of it. With the new arrivals this afternoon, we now number 632, and my job here is to try and keep law and order among you all; to see that, as far as I possibly can, everyone is treated fairly. We are all in the same boat, and I'm sure you don't need me to tell you that! Every one of you has a perfect right to come and see me at any time – day or night – and I will try to help you in any way that is open to me. That I promise you!"

He paused to let his words sink in, and a little ripple of interest ran through his listening audience.

"Now I know," he went on, "that is difficult for some of you adjust to life of captivity, life in a prison camp, but we must all help each other in this. If we do this, and act reasonably and with common sense, we shall manage very well. Of that I am sure! I have put you new fellows in huts six and seven. No doubt some of you have already palled up while you have been moving around, and if this is so, there is no reason why you should be split up. The first thing to do is to elect a hut leader, and he will be responsible for what goes on in the hut. He will be the first person you turn to for advice, or if you have a complaint. He should do his best to help. If he cannot, then he comes to me and I will do my best to sort things out. Failing this, the individual can come along and see me himself. Okay?"

Lt. Schroder was an entirely different kind of man to Kohler of the last camp. This little speech, whilst differing little from what Kohler had said, was given with a great deal more personal dignity and assurance. Every man present felt that Schroder would, indeed, do all that he could for each man there, and at the same time, he would do it with justice, and without any watchful or wary look being kept upon the British reaction.

The German soldier likes to feel that someone oversees any situation. Someone in authority, who uses that authority with care and discretion. Every man present felt that Schroder would do just this. He was what the Germans like to think of as the 'typical' German officer, and what the British like to think of as the 'better type' of German officer. Thus, both sides were happy with their choice.

Schroder's officers were busy handing around some papers. "Now I should like you to fill these in. If you will," Schroder said. "Just your name, date of birth, home address, military unit, and so on... No, don't worry. We are not giving military information to the enemy. They probably know more than we do anyway. This is mainly for our own purposes to start with, and then I'm sure that some of you will want to get a message home to your families to let them know that you are still alive. We are permitted, by the Red Cross, to send home one letter or lettercard per month, and I would like to get this on the way for you as soon as possible."

A murmur of approval went around at this. The question of whether their families knew they were still alive and in reasonable health was one that caused a great deal of anxiety among the prisoners.

Schroder spoke again. "Finally, one last thing. Camp 29 is a labour camp, which means all that are fit to do so will work. The work is mainly on the land, and you will go in groups of some twenty or twenty-five men. In a day or two you will be told which working parties you are to belong to, and what you are to do. That's all! Oh! And just in case some of you have lost count of the days, tomorrow is Sunday! Goodnight to you all!"

And he left the dining hall.

"Labour camp?" Herbert queried silently. This took some time to sink in. They were, after all, still soldiers, and why should they help their enemy on the 'home front' from working on the land? They had not expected this. "Well bloody damn," said one chap. "I'm not working for them. Not bloody likely. I'll report sick in the morning and stop in bed for the next few weeks. If this bloody war doesn't last too much longer, I can stay in bed until the end…"

"Balls!" came the reply.

Alfred was a bit mixed up about the work himself. He had no more desire to help the British than any other German soldier, but as he said to Herbert, "If we kick up a shindy and refuse to work, what'll happen? We shall get punished one way or other. And if we do what we are told, and go to work on the land, I don't suppose we shall be helping them all that much, and we might as well get out and about a bit. See something other than bloody barbed wire. See something of the farms, and the countryside. Almost anything would be better than this constant aimless wandering about inside a compound."

Herbert was inclined to agree. "After all, it is at the enemy's expense," he said. "We might as well make the best of it and see as much as we can."

"I've talked myself into this," Alfred grinned. "I'm quite looking forward to it." His face took on a sort of glazed look.

"There might even be some women," he said. "There might even be a chance of…"

"My God," Herbert was aghast. "Don't think of fraternising. That's against everyone's rules, both sides. You won't half put a cat among the pigeons."

"Rubbish!" Alfred's grin nearly split his face in half.

"You'll do the same, given half the chance. Anyone would, so shut up!"

"You got sex on the brain, mate."

Alfred nodded. "Well, it was food! But that meal in the dining hall satisfied that… temporarily. So now it's not food that's uppermost in my mind at the moment…."

After all the papers had been completed, Hut 71 selected Sergeant Weber to be their chief. He said he didn't know what he was letting himself in for, but he would 'have a go' and do his best.

This seemed to settle all the routine matters for the time being, so Herbert clambered on to his top bunk, and in seconds was sleeping the sleep of the just.

Next day, after the usual roll-call, Hut 7 was kept busy. First there was the issue of the chocolate coloured tunics with the bright coloured squares and circles sewn on to them which had so astonished Herbert upon his arrival. Now he was wearing them himself. The trade mark! The badge, the emblem, the symbol of his captivity. He began to feel conspicuous and uncomfortable, but not so Alfred. He immediately gave an impromptu fashion show. "Look!" he said, mincing up and down, his hand on his stocky hip. "See what Alfred is wearing this year. Note the delightful shade of warm sludge, highlighted here and there by appliquéd circles! My dear, it's the only possible thing for Nissen hut wear! It's bound to catch on. In no time everyone will be wearing it!"

They were given working tunics, boots, ground sheet, underwear, and last off, a kit-bag to keep the lot in. It reminded Herbert of the kitting out of raw recruits when he had first joined the German army. But... this was from a far different angle.

In the afternoon, a civilian photographer arrived at the camp. For one blissful moment, Herbert, who rather enjoy having his photograph taken, thought it was a kind gesture, a service provided for sending home of photographs to Mother. But it wasn't. It was for the prisoner's record.

Everyone was given a number, and from then on, referred to by this means only. Herbert found he was no longer Herbert Baum-Hacker of Hamburg, but Prisoner A/956378, and he promptly learned it off by heart.

He had no wish to miss out on anything that was going on simply because he did not recognise his own number. He rather felt that he would be hearing it a lot in the next few weeks, and the first thing he was told to do was mark it upon all his clothes and possessions.

The new arrivals, dressed in their new issue of prison clothing, were lined up to be photographed, one by one. They were instructed to stand in front of a white sheet, which was supported by two poles. A piece of white card, with their number on it, was to be held across their chest. Then a further photograph was taken in profile this time, with the number card held sideways.

The photographer, rather overcome with his task, got a bit carried away really, and repeatedly asked everybody to smile before he clicked the shutter. Alfred obliged, and asked if a background of potted plants could be there, but perhaps fortunately, the photographer did not understand his German. A sickly grin was the best that most of them could manage, which then disappeared immediately.

Alfred made judicious enquires about whether he could purchase a couple of prints, perhaps an enlargement. He thought if he could send one home to Germany, it would show his wife what was being worn in England this year. It might even be a new trend in Germany. It would certainly give C&A a headache.

Back in Hut 7, Herbert had time to take stock of his new hut-mates. They came from all walks of life, from all parts of Germany. There were garage mechanics, a butcher, schoolmasters, bank clerks, office boys, a publican, a couple of plumbers, a tailor, several factory workers, hotel porters, a taxi driver, a dental assistant, and a few professional soldiers. Then, of course the inevitable 'Mummy's boys' who had never done anything before they were called up and were forced to mix with the rough soldiery. In a strange and obscure way, you could almost feel sorry for them. They were all sorts, that back home in Germany would be wearing pure silk pyjamas and having their nails regularly manicured.

They were the sybarites, the parasites, the ultra fastidious. The ones upon whom no responsibility had ever developed beyond being on time for dinner; who had never been forced to earn their own living. Their lives had been cushioned and cloistered to an unnatural degree, and now here they were, thrown down among as motely an assortment as you could find, everyone of whom would undoubtedly put them right if they stepped one foot out of line.

By some strange quirk of fate, these types always seemed to manage to stay clear of the dirtier bits of war. True, they could not pursue their normal way of life, but they seemed mostly to end up in the pay corps or in one of the catering units, and seldom, if ever, saw the carnage of front line fighting.

'Well!' Herbert made a mental note. 'We're all in this lot together now, whatever were in civilian life. We shall get served the same way. Some of us will survive very well. Alfred will certainly emerge unscathed. We're all lumped together, so we shall just have to all bloody well get along together. Whatever we were once, we're all the same now…'

One of the camp officials arrived with the promised postcards, and one was issued to each prisoner so that they could send word home. It was rather a strange sensation to have a pencil in his hand again, Herbert thought, and pondered upon the small area of card in front of him. His prisoner number had to come first, in the left-hand corner. Having a number rather than a name made him feel a bit like a criminal. He had never actually been one!

There was not very much room on the postcard, and in any case they all had been warned to be careful about what they wrote. Any doubts about the message, and the cards would not be sent. Herbert therefore restricted himself to an innocuous message telling his mother that he was alright, quite safe, and in good health, and that he hoped all the rest of the family was too. Regards to his friends etc. and she was not to worry.

He reflected that by the time all the postcards had been checked over by Camp Intelligence, and sent via Switzerland to Germany, the news they contained would be a bit stale anyway. But he felt a great relief that he was able to get some news to his family. They might have some official notification, but if not, his mother would have worried herself a wreck by now. Anyway, he'd done his best. There was damn all else he could do now.

Three days later, Herbert was on his way back to work. Sitting in the back of a lorry, with nineteen others, and guarded by three British guards. What a caper this was. The lorry had seen better days... and a long time ago. It trundled its way along bumpy twisting lanes, braking every so often so that everyone in the back lost their balance. The exhaust pipe, if it still existed, appeared to be suffering from some malfunction and filled the lorry with nauseous fumes.

The lorry ground to a juddering halt in what appeared to be a farmyard, and Herbert wished that he had better command of the English language. It irritated him not to be able to understand what was being said around him. The few words he had already picked up were insufficient to enable him to realise what the farmer was saying to the guards, but one thing seemed clear enough. The prisoners were there to work.

'Right! Let's get at it,' thought Herbert. He was torn between the real desire to get on with some work for the first time in weeks, especially as he rather enjoyed physical work, and it would be a relief from the stifling boredom of hanging out in the camp, and an innate loyalty to Germany. The good German soldier does not help the enemy, even by digging ditches. On the other hand, he had the normal stranger's curiosity about England, and the English way of life, and felt he would like to look around and learn what he could.

"Oh, Christ! Forget it," he told himself. "Do as you're told and play it by ear. What the hell?"

One chap was detailed to be cook and was left with the instructions to erect a kitchen, make a fire, and start getting the meal ready for mid-day. Herbert felt sure that they had, as usual, picked the most unsuitable bloke of all to be cook. They always did. The system was usually just to point a finger without making any preliminary enquiries as to whether the chap had ever known how to boil water before! Anyway, all they were supposed to have some bread, cheese and margarine, washed down with tea made with dried milk, all brought with them from the camp. However, perhaps if the farmer could be chatted up by one of the guards, he could scrounge a few potatoes to make weight! It would be quite gratifying if the cook could produce such an acceptable meal, and he seemed to show some faint enthusiasm. By the time he had collected the wood for the fire, which was not as dry as it should be, got the damn thing going, peeled the spuds, divided the rations into the mathematically exact portions demanded by the German soldiery, he had his hands pretty full.

On balance, Herbert decided that the job of being a cook did not appeal. It was not so easy as if the first appeared, and he would not volunteer for such duties. Let some other poor sod get the boos and catcalls if he couldn't make up a decent cup of tea.

The prisoners were spread out along the edge of the field and ordered to start digging. Rumour had it that there had once been a ditch there, but they found this hard to believe. Shovels, spades and pick-axes had been supplied, and delivered in advance to the site. They seemed to be brand new, but had an alien look about them, at least to German eyes.

Apparently not. This was the standard length of handle for English tools, they were told, and they were curtly ordered to get on with the work and shut up complaining. They picked up the tools, and the work got started, the guards taking it in turns to patrol along the length of the ditching gang. It was quite pleasant really, out in the fresh air, getting some proper exercise. Well, almost anything was better than the aimless total boredom of wandering around the camp compound, sitting on the hut steps, leaning in against the corners, lying on your bunk. Talking for the sake of talking and walking about just to make your legs move.

The question of a lavatory soon arose. The guard who was hovering around the cook was summoned to attend their prisoner who demanded this non-existent amenity, and he was ordered to keep him in sight and make sure he did not scarper. The prisoner took exception to this. "I'm not going with him.

I'm not having his rifle pointing at my bare arse...."

The guards consulted together, and it was decided that two prisoners should be detailed to construct a 'donnerbalken'. Obviously as they were going to be working there for most of the day, something would have to be provided. They were ordered to make it central to the working party so that the guards would not need to escort everybody and could keep all the prisoners in view. A square hole of about two feet by three feet was dug out, and two forked sticks, from the hedge, were driven to the ground, one at either end. A four-foot sapling, about six inches thick, was then cut and places across resting in the forks, and the 'donnerbalken' was ready for 'blast off!'

As the day wore on, there was no shortage of customers. As long you kept your feet on balance, let your feet dangle, and over you would go. A bit hard on the short-assed ones! Toilet paper was not supplied outside if the camp, so a good supply of grass was a further necessity.

Back at the camp, the day's happenings were well taken over among the prisoners. Some of them still had reservations about 'helping the enemy' but the way Herbert looked at it, he had helped himself. He felt fatigued, in fact he felt damn right tired, but it was the healthy kind of tired feeling, not the stiff boredom tired. The physical work had seemed to put the use back into the muscles, and the fresh air, and a change of scenery had made him feel a great deal better. Depending on the farms, the farmers and the guards, on balance most of the working parties seemed to have had a good day.

And so, the days went on. If it turned wet, and rained for more than an hour, they returned to the camp without further work. Their main difficulty was to somehow contrive to get warm, and to dry themselves and their clothing ready for the following day.

Friday was pay day, and if all had gone well, and there had not been too much wet weather, a grand total of one shilling could be earned. So, on Fridays, after five days of work, you were relatively rich. The money was paid out to each prisoner in the form of round plastic discs and were almost all spent Friday night in the canteen, on a few cigarettes, a piece of fruit cake, some drawing paper, razor blades, shoe polish or similar luxuries. Five shillings did not take much time to spend, and Fridays became something to look forward to, a real highlight in the week.

Everyone had different priorities. Peter Bauer, a tall thin cadaverous looking chap, was a very heavy smoker. Up until now, he had been forced to curtail himself, for there were very few fags to be obtained, and as a result, he was irritable, bad-tempered and touchy. But now he was earning, he was back in business. He could buy fags. With his five shillings, provided he hadn't rained too often, he could buy sixty cigarettes. This was not a week's supply. Not to anyone who smoked as much as Peter Bauer, so with true German thoroughness, he dealt with the matter.

With a borrowed a razor blade (borrowed because he had given up shaving and did not propose to spend his fag money on blades), he cut each cigarette lovingly into a little tin, he thus had one hundred and eighty cigarettes, each a third of the length of a normal one. Dividing this total onto seven days (five working days, a Saturday and a Sunday in camp), he could smoke twenty-five a day, and thirty on Sunday. That'll have to do it, he thought. But he would adhere strictly to his calculations, or preferably, smoke twenty-four and save one each day, just in case there were weeks when he could not buy the whole sixty.

Somehow or another, no one ever knew exactly, how he managed to purloin an old table knife, and he fashioned it into a very acceptable woodworking tool. With this, he carefully carved a cigarette holder out of a fragment of the boxwood which he had found one day whilst working on one of the local farms. So, by this means, he managed to smoke his one-third length cigarettes down to the very last shred of tobacco.

Herbert and Alfred didn't bother too much about cigarettes. Alfred liked the odd one occasionally, but Herbert was a non-smoker. They spent their money on food. Friday night was, for them, 'cake night' and with their working out in the open air, they seemed to be permanently hungry. The cake was not even particularly good cake. Made with powdered milk and dried eggs, it was a particularly virulent shade of yellow, but the sickly sweetness of it seemed to be what they needed just at the time. Herbert rather remembered the linzertorte they had eaten at home on high-days and holidays, and great slabs of rum soaked sticky fruit cake. But, for the moment, this would have to do.

He and Alfred talked over their finances as if they were well-established stockbrokers. They apportioned out their plastic discs with great care and would discuss at some length the merits of an extra piece of cake, against making the last razor blade last another week. They planned it out so that they would not spend all but would just keep a little aside in case they got a wet week and could not go to work. But then, Alfred would suddenly say, "Tonight's the night for a bank raid, my old friend! Tonight we feast!" And so, they did, and had to start saving all over again.

Klaus Kellner was an ordinary sort of chap. At least he had always seemed so. He was of medium build, with red hair, and the kind of pale complexion that usually goes with that colouring. He was quiet, spoke little, and that in a soft well-modulated voice. He was not sulky, or argumentative, and seemed to fit in well with the other prisoners in his hut. Then, quite suddenly and without any warning, he 'got religion.' He became totally convinced that he had received 'the call' and had been chosen to preach the good book to all and sundry – namely his fellow prisoners. This idea became firmly fixed in his head, and nothing would fix it.

He let his hair grow long, and in this age of cropped heads, his mane of copper locks looked distinctly odd. He gave up shaving, and soon had a full reddish tinged beard. He managed, by begging, borrowing or stealing, to obtain a spare blanket, and from this he fashioned a monkish robe, tied around his middle with a rope. He made himself some thonged sandals from the shoelaces and remains of old boots, and thus garbed he was nothing so much as a 'stand-in for Isiah' as Herbert said.

He wrote out such bits of the Bible that he could remember, or force anyone else to remember, and he bound them together with two bits of cardboard. Armed with this, he went from hut to hut attempting to preach, adopting a parsonical resonant tone of voice, and punctuating his well-turned phrases with elaborate arm sweeping gestures. He would plead with them all to pray with him, and stand in the middle of the hut, his eyes turned heavenwards, his beard jutting aggressively, and his arms upraised so that his wide sleeves fell back along his rather skinny and none too clean arms.

Most of the time, he was kicked out, either verbally, or even sometimes physically, but he bore no malice. He forgave them, he said, as he picked himself up from the ground outside the huts, and he inevitably returned later.

He became the subject of the most outrageous ribaldry, the butt of all the smutty jokes, but he accepted it all with total calmness and an air of almost saint-like peace. Herbert thought at first, he was 'having them on', that this was just a big act, but as time went on, and he had the opportunity to observe Klaus, he realised that the man was in deadly earnest. He was really trying, and with it all, he seemed to have acquired a new strange sort of peace, of acceptance, or perhaps of entirely disregard, the personal abuse of his fellow prisoners.

And there was no doubt about it, he really did have a flair for it. Just occasionally, only very occasionally, someone would listen to him, and he could really talk. He knew just what he was about. In time, he came to be known as 'Jesus from Hut 7' and in his appearance and manner, he grew more and more like one of the ancient prophets.

The hut leader asked him one day what the idea was, and Klaus replied with serenity that people were not all the same. Even when confined together as they were all in close captivity, some could cope better than others. Some needed extra help, extra comfort and guidance to enable them to survive. He, Klaus, felt that he had been called upon to provide this. He felt that he could help, and that was really all he wished to do. There was as yet, no camp priest or parson, and somebody had to make a start somewhere. He felt that even if he seemed to be doing no good, he was certainly doing no harm, and perhaps someone, somewhere along the way could be made to feel better by listening to him, Klaus. And he added sharply, "It wouldn't hurt you to come along and hear me preach sometime, either."

The Hut Leader was unrepentant.

"Push off," he said.

Conrad Ullrich had been a corporal in the Panzer Corps, and he was quite a brainy sort of chap. Reasonably good looking, too. Tall and slim with one of those fresh-looking faces that always look clean and seemed to please everyone. Herbert privately called 'Ruritanian' a bit like the Prisoner of Zenda, but he never said so, in case Conrad took exception to the description. He could talk the hind leg off a donkey, and the animal would stand happily listening upon its remaining three. He was not a 'big head', for he wouldn't have lasted long with this crowd if he had been, but he was reasonably well-educated and knowledgeable.

He could talk about many things in a way that was neither pedantic nor dogmatic. He never went out of his way to gather his fellows around him, he merely remained where he was, and they unfailingly sought him out. Each night, a small crowd would collect around his bunk, and the buzz of conversation would be enlivened with sporadic bursts of laughter.

One evening, Herbert and Alfred went among the group talking to Conrad when, without warning one of the chaps let rip a tremendous fart! It was not merely the casual breaking of wind, it was a clarion call, a heralding of storm to come, and it echoed around the walls of the hut, ricocheting from the walls, and reverberating like cannon fire.

"Mein Gott," said a little bloke in tones of awe and wonder, "Did you have to do that? It's a good job you don't shoot out flames as well..."

The offender feigned nonchalance, Conrad, as usual, was equal to the occasion. "What a complete waste of methane gas," he said, grinning.

"Did you know that the gasses in the human body give off a beautiful blue flame when set alight?"

The information was received in silence. "Oh! Yes! They do indeed," he continued. "If only it could somehow be bottled and conserved for future use, we should all make a fortune!"

The crowd was sceptical, "I don't believe it, mate. A fart is a fart is a fart.... And that's all there is to it." Conrad sought to prove his point. "Friends, gather around," he said. "I will personally prove to you, beyond any shadow of doubt, that a build up of wind pressure in my body – otherwise known colloquially as a 'fart' – will when released, and lit by an ordinary match, burn like a gas flame. The size of the flame obviously depends upon human body temperature... and with the amount of carbohydrates we are all being forced to eat, at the moment... Now, if you don't mind gazing fixedly at my hairy bottom..."

He removed his trousers and underwear and lay down upon his bunk. "I shall now concentrate on building up my body pressure," he explained. One of his own particular cronies, Kurt stood at alert with a match.

"Don't put the match too close in case it backfires," somebody suggested. With a few coarse breaths, his face was becoming distinctly flushed. He closed his eyes. Seconds went by, and his face took on a faint purple hue. Suddenly he shouted "Match Kurt!" and, lifting both legs into the air with a wild swing, he let fly with a blast that nearly very matched the first one.

The match, operated by a very wary Kurt was held about three inches away from the seat of the explosion, produced a twelve-inch blue and green flame, maintained, as Conrad said, by human body gas. He had proved his point.

Alfred gave it as his opinion that this was a bit too close for comfort, and far too close to the 'essential' area. He would not have a flame that close to his arse, he said. Most of the hut seemed to think the whole thing howlingly funny, and some kind of a new game. It soon caught on, and one of two from the less nimble, more clumsy ones, suffered scorch marks over the next few days. The thing was ended by the simple fact that they all ran out of matches.

Camp 29 had been settled down quite well by now. Things had fallen into place, and a general routine had become established, for which Herbert was personal grateful for. One of the worst aspects of being prisoner was knowing what you would do for all the hours that you actually spent locked in behind barbed wire. Okay so you could go and lie down in your bunk bed and read; you could chat to your mates, but then what? People got irritated and fed up with each other and with themselves. The conversation would take a turn for the worse, stray onto delicate subjects which could catch the listener on the raw, and even end up in a punch-up, with fellow hut-mates, attempting to drag the participants apart before the Lagerführer or one of the camp officials heard the row, and found it necessary to take some action.

Food and provision of enough of it took a great deal of their thoughts, and after that, sex, or the absence of it in any form, predominated. In both areas, they were hungry.

It seemed necessary, for the general welfare and morale of the camp, to be organising something, to get some people involved in some kind of plan, to be actually constructing or making, to awaken some kind of interest in something; in fact, anything. Camp 29 had the usual football teams, and games were played in all weathers, especially in the evening when the prisoners returned from work, and at weekends. Some of the men even contrived makeshift tennis rackets from pieces of wood. Not exactly to Slazenger standard, it is true, and they would certainly cause raised eyebrows at Wimbledon, but they served as a twofold purpose. The art and skill in their manufacture, and the invention of various games that could be played with them afterwards.

One hut on the camp remained empty. No one could find out whether it was destined to be used in the future, whether a further intake was expected, or whether it had been set aside for some unspecified, and as yet unfilled purpose. In any event, it seemed a criminal waste to allow that room to stand idle.

A few of the prisoners formed a deputation to the Lagerführer to see if he could obtain permission to convert this as yet empty hut into a camp theatre so that they could put on some entertainments. He promised to see the commandant, and to do his best to persuade him. At length, after many consultations with the British officer, a rather wary permission was given. A notice appeared in the dining-hall asking for the names of those who would be interested in forming a theatre; not only those who could actually perform, or do a 'turn', but carpenters, electricians, and anyone who was good with their hands. They also wanted some of them to have ago and writing suitable material, short plays, monologues, sketches. The notice said, 'anyone and anything considered' and the response was terrific.

Before joining the army, Herbert had been a member of an amateur theatrical group in Hamburg for about four years, and he had therefore quite a lot of experience. The world of theatre fascinated him. He loved the air of excitement, the smell of greasepaint, the peppery dusty chalky smell behind the scenes. He loved the feel of the stage, the sound of his own feet on the wooden boards, the fantasy, the make-believe. He had nurtured no ambition to actually earn his living in the theatre; he was sufficiently realistic to know that it was precarious at the best of times, but he had been successful in one of two small unambitious plays that the local group had produced.

In retrospect, he often felt that these must have been the happiest times of his life. The fun that they had at rehearsals, the learning of the lines, sometimes not without difficulty, the good acting and awful acting, the 'hammering', the drying up the prompting. The wrong coloured spotlights, wavery stage sets, with paint either too thick or thin layers. The middle-aged woman who was their make-up artist, and who always wanted to make your nose look longer with stage 'putty'; to age you with thick black lines across your forehead. If not watched with great care, and handled with supreme diplomacy, she would have put false pimples, warts and scabs all over everybody, whether the part called for it or not! And after rehearsals, the frothing beer they all felt they had truly earned. The laughter, the unity, the sense of accomplishing something... Herbert was undoubtedly hooked on applause. He could hear it in his head now. You stood on stage, down centre. You were so nervous, your mouth had all dried up, and you couldn't have spat if you tried. In front of you, a sea of white faces, that just momentarily, you regarded as hostile. Suddenly, words rushed into your mouth. You grow taller. They laugh, and applaud, and you know you have them in the palm of your hand. They are on your side. Oh. Yes! Herbert was going to offer his services, he could hardly wait, and as Alfred was a carpenter by trade, he dragged him along too.

Fritz Reimers was the one who actually thought up the idea of the theatre project and put the notice in the dining hall. He had been vainly casting about for something in which virtually the whole camp could become excited, something that would perhaps generate a little excitement, lift them up all up a bit, and help to shake off the mental lethargy with which they suffered spasmodically. He was a professional actor, from Berlin, and he went on about the whole business with German thoroughness, making detailed notes of what every one of the volunteers could offer.

In about four days flat, the group was formed. Then it was necessary to once again approach the British camp commandant to see if they could be allowed the use of a few tools, like hammers, saw, nails, a bit of paint etc. They made a list. A very long list, and by the time the British officers looked all the way down it, they allowed half of it. "Well! It's not a bad start," Fritz said philosophically. "We've asked the blokes in the kitchen to save us all the cardboard boxes, so that should help. Don't worry, you chaps! We'll have this show on the road in no time. And we'll invite the Tommies to the first night performance, and that may help a little."

One thing that caused some delay was that the tools which the group had been allowed to have had to be handed in at the main gate every night, before lights out, which meant that they could not continue to work as long as they wished.

"I suppose they're afraid we shall build a secret weapon here at night, or something," Alfred's tone was derisory.

"Now! I ask you! What harm would it do to let us go on a hammer and a few nails?"

"Well you know what say…." Herbert quoted, "Give an Italian a weapon, and he won't know what to do with it. Give a German an empty tin can, and he will make a tank out of it…"

Alfred snorted unconvinced.

In a relatively short few weeks, the transformation of the empty hut into a camp theatre was almost complete. The effect was, to put it mildly, fantastic and all built from virtually nothing. A stage had been provided, with curtains made from dark red sack cloth. There were footlights which could be dimmed, and spotlights. They had thought of almost everything and had scrounged every bit of wherewithal to provide it. Where most of it originated from, no one thought it advisable to ask.

The next problem to be overcome was that of music, and the instruments upon which to make it. Once again, the Lagerführer approached the British commandant, and eventually an ancient, rather out of tune bar-room piano was delivered to the camp. B-flat and E-minor were missing, never to be heard again, but the time the camp musicians had had a go at it, it was almost as good as grand! Almost! One of the prisoners made a guitar out of a thin wooden box, once again 'lifted' from heaven knows where, but it looked quite reasonable when he had finished it. What they wanted now, more than anything else, was a drum kit.

What can be achieved with empty tea chests and empty marmalade tins had to be seen to be believed. And they didn't stop short on the trimmings either. Side drums, cymbals mounted on top, castinettes, tom-toms – the lot. After some practise, the little band began to play quite well together, and were ready to perform in public.

On New Year's Eve 1945, the show called 'Variety from All Over The World' opened. The British commandant with some of his officers, sat in the seat of honour in the front row, and gave every evidence of thoroughly enjoying the performance.

Fortunately, their German was not good enough to understand the many ad-libs and asides at their expense, and although the Lagerführer laughed with all the others, he got just a stiff-necked towards the end. At the conclusion of the show, the British commandant made a little speech, publicly congratulating them all on the performance, which he said he greatly enjoyed, and particularly upon the successful transformation of an empty hut into a theatre. He had not seen it until tonight, he said, and he had been astonished at what they had been able to achieve. A real triumph of ingenuity.

The show, and indeed the project, was undoubtedly a success, a real triumph. Fritz Reimers, who had many triumphs on the real stage, felt that none of them had meant more to him than this one, performed in such conditions, against over-whelming odds. He was jubilant.

The morale of the camp had improved by leaps and bounds, and the whole atmosphere was brisker. Fritz decided there would be no time lag. They must not be allowed to fall back, so he planned to put on two one-act plays written by the prisoners themselves, and rehearsals were to begin immediately. Alfred detailed the new stage scenery, and Herbert was given his lines to learn.

"No resting on your laurels," Fritz exhorted them all. "Let's keep this pot boiling." And so they did.

All the prisoners, without exception, enjoyed the evenings at the camp theatre. It was always full to capacity, and as time went on, the original theatre group expanded so as to involve more and more of the men.

News from home was so scarce as to be almost non-existent. They had no news of the war that had brought them here, but just for a few hours each week, they could inhabit some kind of fantasy world; they could be busy and important. They could tax their ingenuity to its utmost limits. They could feel that they were all together working towards a common end, even if that end was in reality only the putting on of a very corny show to entertain themselves. It would be untrue to say that this 'made them happy'. It did not, for they were not happy. They were not free, they could not come and go as they chose; they were totally uninformed, and knew nothing of what was going on outside the camp. For the most part they were filled with anxiety about their wives, their families left back home in Germany.

They knew of the heavy air raids. They sometimes heard aircraft in the night, and for all they knew their homes could be a flattened heap of rubbish, with everything that they held dear buried beneath it.

But to think along those lines was certain despair. This was for the second and third tier of thought. The first tier, and the only one that made life tenable these days, was mere surface thoughts about today: What they would have to eat, how the show would go, whether it would rain or not. Do not think of yesterday, and certainly not of tomorrow. Just keep on being, and keeping busy. Fill every daylight hour; do not allow time for your brain to slip from the first tier on to the second. Tire yourself out, mentally and physically. If, in the dark, private enwrapped hours of the night, second or third tier thoughts flash on the screen behind your eyes, sheer fatigue must blot them out. This imprisonment had to be borne, for there was no way out. They just had to make it endurable, and wear it into shape. Herbert was one of those who, at least on the first tier was 'happy'. He was 'on the boards' again, and how he revelled in it.

Some weeks later, when the daily working parties were returned to the camp, they dispersed to their huts, all exactly as usual, but the sight that met their eyes when they flung open the door, stopped their chat instantly, and stunned them into total silence. The ones first through the doors were brought to an abrupt halt, and the ones following crowded in, trying to see over their shoulders. The entire contents of each and every hut had been thoroughly turned over, and everything that the hut had contained was piled into a heap in its centre.

The chaos was unbelievable. "Mein Gott!" Herbert said, when he found his voice. "What the bleeding..." Then he looked at Alfred, to find Alfred looking at him.

"The theatre," they said in unison, and ran.

The camp theatre had suffered the same fate. The only thing remaining in its original place was the red sackcloth curtaining, hanging forlornly. Fast as they had been, Fritz

106

Reimers was there before them, and in a sad and sorry state. He sat on a broken stool, his head in his hands, his shoulders slumped in dejection. He did not answer when they spoke to him. The whole place was a shambles. It had taken weeks to put it into order, and this had been considered fairly quick, for they had worked hard, and with the speed of new-found enthusiasm, but it had taken less than half a day to wreak total havoc.

Just then roll-call was sounded, and afterwards, the Lagerführer spoke to them. He was careful to keep his tone even. "We have been invaded today by a special group of British soldiers detailed to make an intensive search of this camp, and this accounts for the disorder you found in your huts. I know it is going to take you all some time to get it sorted out, but it must be done, and without delay. What this special group were looking for, nobody knows, but the British commandant here assures me that nothing was discovered, and nothing removed."

There was a great deal of muttering among the assembled prisoners, and a bit of 'Bloody cheek' and 'What the hell' but the attitude of the Lagher Führer, and his factual tone, helped to calm them down. It took Hut 7 more than three hours just to sort out their belongings, and for weeks afterwards, people were still swapping boots, underclothing and blankets. The theatre took longer to put back to rights, but Fritz Reimers decided not to wait until it was accomplished. He felt it was necessary to keep the theatre project going, and not allow the men to lapse back. To go 'off the boil' as he put it, so he called rehearsals for the following night, amid the confusion.

The next few weeks passed in comparative peace and quiet, and the tenor of the camp returned to normal, but Hut 16 had not forgotten the intrusion. It seemed to rankle with them, and they gave a great deal of thought to 'getting their own back' in some way. They wanted to 'thumb their nose' at the British, but couldn't quite think of how to do this.

Eventually, though, they had an idea, but they kept very quiet about it, and said nothing to anybody. That is until April 20th, the birthday of Adolph Hitler, the Führer.

Hut 16 acquired, by what means no one ever found out, a white sheet and some pillow cases from the hospital hut. From other quarters a supply of red ink had been organised. The inmates set to work, and in a short time their self-inflicted task was complete. They had manufactured a German Swastika flag, about six foot by three foot, and accurate in every detail. As dawn broke on April 20th, this flag was flying high from the top of the water tower in the very centre of Camp 29. It was a beautiful sight, and Hut 16 glowed with a sense of achievement.

Roll-call was earlier that morning, and as everyone turned out of their huts, moaning and grumbling because of the unexpected change in the routine, they were met with this glorious sight. They paused, and blinked, still half-asleep. Then they pointed it out to each other, and a great roar went up. The entire camp burst into ribald laughter. It laughed uproariously, it held its sides, and slapped itself on the back. Just for a few moments, it really did enjoy itself.

The British commandant, of course, was not pleased. Nor was he laughing. One of the Tommies was ordered to remove the offending object, and as he clambered up the tower, and tore down the rag, he was greeted by a prolonged round of applause from the prisoners assembled below.

The culprits must be caught and punished, the commandant told the assembly. "Oh God! Here we go again," Herbert said silently, remembering Auguste Ackerman. The commandant wanted those responsible to own up, to come forward. He would wait for them to do so. "He'll wait a long time..." muttered Alfred. And the camp was dismissed.

Half an hour later, roll-call was sounded again. Herbert and Alfred dropped everything, and set off at a trot.

108

"Christ," said Herbert. "I wish everybody would leave everything alone. Just when things are going smooth, some joker has to start something else... and we shall all have to pay!"

"Perhaps they won't bother..." Alfred was hopeful.

"Of course they'll bother. The British commandant will have to answer to somebody up higher for letting the Swastika fly above his camp, and we shall have to answer to him."

"Perhaps nobody else saw it! He could deny all knowledge..."

"Don't be so bloody daft" Herbert was disgruntled. "That's not likely is it?" Herbert was right. The whole camp had to work for two weeks without pay. No canteen, no wages, no sport or games of any kind.

No privileges at all for two weeks. And no theatre!

"Well, it could have been worse, mate," said one of the inmates of Hut 7 to Herbert as they were dismissed. Herbert didn't think so!

"Piss off!" he said.

One morning, shortly after this, the camp was not dismissed as usual after roll-call, and the British commandant addressed the assembled prisoners through an interpreter.

"The war is over," he said. "Germany has been defeated, and has surrendered. England and the Allies have won the war." The voice stopped. The camp stood absolutely still and in silence. They were momentarily stunned by the baldness of the announcement, and they did not know how to take it, or what reaction was expected of them.

Then quite suddenly a voice at the back said "Bloody good job! Now perhaps we can all go home!" and the tension seemed to break.

'It can't happen that quick' Herbert made a mental reservation. 'Not just like that. Red tape and everything... it'll be months before they send us back...'

The interpreter continued, "All prisoners of war will be politically screened today. This will be carried out in strict rotation, starting with Hut No.1. Our Intelligence officers are already in the dining hall, and they will question you individually. Full co-operation is expected from all prisoners. It will be to your own ultimate advantage to give correct information."

The camp was then dismissed and Hut No.1 went to the dining hall to be grilled!

Everyone in Hut 7 seemed to be quite dazed by the announcement that the war was now at an end. They had been without news for a very long time, and had had no means of knowing that the fighting had been drawing to a close. What was meant by political screening? Did anyone know? How long would it be before they could all go home? Was home still there? What would they do with us now? Will they keep these camps going for a bit until things are settled? The questions were bandied about, but no one knew any of the answers.

Then it was Herbert's turn to be 'grilled' in the dining hall, and he found himself standing in front of the intelligence officer.

"POW number?"

Herbert gave it.

"Name? Rank?"

Herbert replied mechanically. Then a lot of personal details.

Who were your friends?

Did you ever know anyone called so and so? Were you ever a member of a group that met at such and such a cafe? And so on. Herbert answered as best he could, he hadn't the slightest idea of what the chap was getting at! Then the officer said, "Did you know that your father has lost his job for being a member of the Nazi Party? That your mother belongs to the party too? You were yourself a member of the Hitler Youth, and so was your brother Fritz!"

Herbert visibly staggered beneath this verbal barrage. 'God!' he thought 'This bloke has done his homework. Why on earth should they have bothered about me? I could hardly be said to be an important part of the Nazi machine?' In any case, he had not heard from home for a long time, and he had no idea of the state of affairs prevailing there at the moment, nor what his father and mother were doing. He did not even know if Fritz was still alive. What the hell was the bloke trying to get at?

The officer gazed at him blandly, and mentally noted his confusion. Then he said, "If you were given a choice, a free choice, would you choose a Nazi Camp or a Democratic Camp?"

'Now, how the hell do I answer that?' Herbert thought. 'What on earth is a Nazi Camp?'

The officer continued, "The Democratic Camp will have great advantages. You could be returned home to Germany sooner than you think."

Herbert couldn't think at all at the moment. He couldn't get over the fact that this unknown British intelligence officer knew so much about him, a mere humble soldier! And why? Everything was happening too fast, and his brain was in a turmoil. All he really wanted was to be able to go home again, to see all the familiar faces and places, but it wasn't going to be like that was it? Nothing was ever going to be the 'old familiar' again. Nothing! The places would probably be bombed ruins, and the faces dead and mouldering in their graves. What the hell should he say? He must speak! He opened his mouth, but hesitated. Too long! The officer lost interest. He looked down and wrote something on the papers in front of him. Neat pointed writing, Herbert noted with detached interest. Nice fountain pen too. Held neatly in a well-shaped hand.

"Nazi Camp," he said. "Next!"

Herbert went.

Herbert hadn't taken it all in. All the routine and regiment of the past few weeks was now to be rudely swept aside, and he didn't like it. He felt as if he was in limbo again. He looked around for Alfred, and found him waiting for him, leaning against the outer wooden hall of the dining hall, his lips pursed in a soundless whistle. He grinned when he saw Herbert.

"How did you get on?" Herbert asked him. Alfred shrugged, a non-committal jerk of his stocky shoulders.

"Oh! Me? Well, to tell you the absolute truth, my old mate, I hardly knew what the bloke was on about. He seemed to know an awful lot about me, but I couldn't see that it made any difference. He didn't give me much chance to say anything, even if I wanted to. He went on and on... So! Well, I'm afraid I got a bit worked up and lost my temper. I gave the Nazi salute! It seems like they've put me down for the Nazi Camp."

He stood sharply to attention, clicked his heels, and parodied the goose step. "Me too," said Herbert. "Although God knows what they mean by a Nazi Camp. Looks like I'm stuck with you for a bit longer then?"

"Cheer up, or shut up!" said Alfred, and gave him a playful punch in the gut.

A few weeks later, when he returned to camp after the usual day's work, Herbert found a letter from home awaiting him. He took it in his hand, and looked at his mother's familiar handwriting. He was half afraid to open it, half afraid of what news it might contain. Slowly he tore it open, and turning away from the evening chatter, and the larking about in the hut, enclosed in a private silent world of his own, he read his letter.

The last few months of the war had been terrible, his mother wrote. It had been a chaos, a shambles. His father had just walked out from where he had been stationed, and come home. There had been nobody to command him to either go or to stay, so, terrified for news of his home and his wife, he had just set off, and walked and walked until he arrived home, totally exhausted. Fritz had been wounded, not seriously, and was now recovering. As for herself, she was alright, and was only too thankful that it was all over at last. He would be sorry to learn that many of their neighbours had gone, either fled or been killed, and there had been much bomb damage. She was very tired, and food was desperately scarce, but they were managing. All she hoped for now was that he continued to be safe and well, and would soon be sent back home so that they would all be together again, a complete family once more.

One or two bits of the letter had been blackened out by the censor and try as he might, Herbert could not decipher what had been written underneath them. Anyway, it didn't really matter. He read the letter again and again until he could have recited from memory every comma and full stop. At least they were still alive, even Fritz who had been right in the thick of the fighting. To have news from home relieved much of Herbert's inner anxiety, but it also brought with it a wave of desperate and despairing homesickness. As he held the letter in his hand, just for a few moments, he was back at home, in the parlour. There were the heavy lace curtains at the front window, clean and crisp with constant washing, the dark red chenille tablecloth on the heavily-polished table, and a bowl of late blooms from the garden. His father, a tall erect man, sitting in 'his' chair, reading the newspaper, and from the kitchen, the smell of cooking! Dear God, why must he always revert to the smell of food? He could smell it, he could actually smell it! He was very quiet for the rest of the evening, and even Alfred's antics could not draw him out. So they left him alone, but he was over it by morning.

Six weeks later, Herbert and Alfred stood, complete with the kit-bags containing all their belongings, and forty-five other prisoners, by the main gate of the camp. They were once again on the move. The routine and seemingly endless process of emptying the kit-bags and searching through everything was once more gone through, and then they were loaded onto a lorry and headed for the railway station. As they hurtled through the streets, swerving violently on each corner, Herbert caught sight of the name

113

'Royston' and this was the first time since his capture that he had any idea of the name of any of the places they had passed through. 'Royston'! Royston!' he kept on repeating it over to himself, but he was fairly sure he was not pronouncing it aright. Anyway, where on earth was Royston?

Herbert sat opposite Alfred in the locked railway compartment. They had their tunics unbuttoned, and a few were smoking, sharing fags, taking things easy and preparing to sit out yet another tedious journey.

"Well! Where are we going to end up this time?" Herbert spoke his thoughts aloud.

"I don't know, and I don't bloody well care," Alfred said. "Unless..."

"Unless what?"

"Well, the war is over! And you might just discover that this is the secret weapon the British had up their sleeves all this time!"

"What weapon?"

"An amphibious train! On water-bourne rails! And you might just find that it won't stop until it gets to Germany! How about that then…?"

The entire carriage looked at him and with one accord said, "Shut up!"

CHAPTER VI:

Oxfordshire

The train chugged slowly on its way, labouring heavily up inclines, braking heavily down slopes, and meandering through every tiny 'Halt', with occasional pulls and shunts into sidings to let faster and more important trains get past. The carriage seats, upholstered in a dark hairy material gave off clouds of dust, and Herbert, sitting with his back to the engine, his long legs stretched out beneath the seat in front of him, thought he had travelled more miles locked in a bloody railway carriage then ever he had marched on foot when he was on active service.

He gazed morosely at a faded sepia picture on the opposite wall. It was a place called Blackpool, and showed some kind of iron tower perched precariously above an overcrowded beach, where ladies with bobbed hair, and swim suits with legs in, seemed to be running in and out of the sea, with lots of jolly plump children. Herbert didn't think he would like it much, and hoped he would not go there!

The soporific journey eventually came to an end, the carriage doors were unlocked, and they went through the, by now, normal routine of turning out, lining up and being counted. When the guards had satisfied themselves that nobody had hidden in the lavatory, or underneath any of the seats, the column marched off. It was growing dusk, and the few civilians they encountered stared at them with a mixture of curiosity, and hostility. One rather well-built middle-aged lady, wearing a tweed suit with a pleated skirt, and thick lisle stockings, stuck her nose in the air, gazed pointedly in the opposite direction, and almost ran them down as she pedalled furiously on her black iron 'sit up and beg' bicycle.

The column raggedly moved aside, just in time. "Phew!" muttered Alfred. "They should have let her ride up and down the Siegfried Line... the war would have been over quicker..." The march resumed.

After half an hour's marching, and a turn to the left, they were again confronted with the all too familiar barbed wire compound. The outline of the huts loomed heavy in the darkness. There seemed to be only about eight or nine of them. 'Quite small' Herbert thought. 'Perhaps it's just a transit camp.'

The gate swung open and forty-seven new arrivals entered the cage. A hut had been prepared for them, with double bunks arranged in two rows, with a wide gangway between. This time, Herbert got a bottom one, and Alfred the next one to it. "I wonder if it's worthwhile unpacking..." Alfred commented. They looked around them, taking stock.

Just then an elderly chap came into the hut. He had obviously been here for some time, and knew the ropes. "When you've sorted yourselves out..." he began, shaking hands with as many of them as he could reasonably reach "... there's something to eat for you in the kitchen. The rest of the camp have already had theirs, but you arrived late, so you had better come over and fetch it. Alright?"

"This isn't a very big camp, is it?" Herbert questioned him.

"No mate! There's only one hundred and thirty-seven prisoners, and that's including you lot. I should know! I'm the bloody cook, and when they told me that another forty-seven were expected, I had to go and draw rations for you."

"What's it like here?" Alfred said.

"Oh! Not bad. Not bad. There are seven Tommies here, and they live outside the camp. They're not too bad really. That is, if you take care not to upset them. Then, of course, there's our Lagerführer. He's a complete nutter, but harmless. He lives in Hut 6 with three 'staff'. We call them his bodyguards!" He laughed. "The rest of us are billeted in huts one to four, and the rest of the huts are empty. There is another camp, a sister to this one, about twenty-five miles off. That is the main one and all orders and such like come from there."

"What's this camp do in the daytime? Anything?"

"Oh. Yes! They work. Mostly on the farms around. You know, labouring, things like that. Get paid a shilling a day."

"Doesn't sound much different from the one we've just left," Herbert said. "Still it won't be so bad if we are getting paid. Different farms, different farmers... it'll be a change..."

"Well! Don't be long about your grub, you lot," the cook said heading towards the door. "I like to clear up my kitchen before I finish for the night." And he went.

"Sounds like a bloody housefrau," Alfred grinned.

This little 'sister' camp had no dining hall, hut or canteen. You merely grabbed your tin plate, went to the cookhouse and had it filled, then belted back to your hut, and ate sitting on your bunk, or on a stool or anything else you could find. Then you washed up your own plate and utensils. However, the food was not at all bad, and seemed plentiful, which relieved Herbert's fears no end.

He and Alfred had just finished eating, and were trying to make each other go to the washroom, and wash up all their things, when the Lagerführer entered the hut.

The cook was right! He was a nut! Herbert had him sized up in seconds. He was, according to his marking, a staff sergeant in the German army, but at the moment, he had on his prisoner's chocolate brown uniform, with the coloured circles removed and replaced with plain brown material. He had an admiral's band around his hat, four pips on his shoulders, and three rings round the sleeve of his jacket.

"Bloody hell" said Herbert silently. "He's going to take some sorting out. What the hell is he supposed to be...?"

"Staff Sergeant Brandt! I am the Lagerführer here, and wish to welcome you to Camp 31A. We are happy to have

117

you in our community." He beamed at them. "We hope you will settle down and work with us for a better world. Our friends, the British, expect from us that we will do our part in working for them, as prisoners of war. You will join the rest of the community in the morning, and will be driven in omnibuses to work, and at night you will return again to our little 'haven'."

"He's bloody daft," Herbert decided. Did he hear all right? "'Our friends the British' and 'going to work in omnibuses?' 'Our little haven?' Either he's fallen on his head and hurt his brain, or been brainwashed by the Tommies... or I'm in the wrong outfit. Which is it?" He turned to Alfred, who was wearing the bland seraphic expression he donned for suitable occasions. "Here," said Herbert, digging him in the ribs, "How about going to work on an 'omnibus' instead of a stinking old lorry?"

"Never mind the stinking old lorry, mate," Alfred said. "Listen. Haven't you twigged what's happened? You and I should have been sent to a Nazi Camp, shouldn't we? Well, this doesn't sound like one, does it?" His eyes glowed with amusement. "Somebody's slipped up somewhere, and they've sent us to the wrong camp. Just give us one week here, mate. Just one week, and judging by that daft bugger, our Lagerführer, we can be converted too..."

"Not me," said Herbert, flatly. "I'd rather get sent back to Camp 29. If I thought I might end up like him, I'd hang myself in my braces now... and my mother would chuck me out...'

Roll-call was at seven o'clock the next morning, and was taken by one half-awake British sergeant, and a bemused corporal. When they had established to their mutual satisfaction that no one had slipped away, or been spirited away in the night, they saluted the Lagerführer, who stood there beaming upon the whole proceedings, and left. 'I'll bet they're going to get another hour's kip in,' Herbert thought enviously, and for a second allowed his mind to dwell upon the thought of a large double bed, with pillows, and crisp clean sheets. Of privacy, and curtains drawn across the windows, and perhaps even someone in the other half of the bed… The little man inside his head chuckled, and he stifled further thought.

"Working parties assemble at the main gate," came the call through the camp. It was almost eight a.m.

There he was again! Staff Sergeant Brandt! He looked like nothing so much as a robust turkey cock, with his short little legs, rounded belly, and pendulous folds of extraneous skin below his receding jaw. He bustled along, with his arms full of papers, several of which he periodically shed, and they were picked up by one of the 'bodyguards' closely following.

"He really is a daft little bugger," said the waiting Herbert. Brandt beamed upon the assembly.

"Group One will take Omnibus Four, Group Two will take Omnibus Three, and Group Three will take Omnibus Two. The new arrivals, whom I shall call Group Four will take Omnibus One."

Having apparently settled this to his own satisfaction, if no one else's, he shuffled once more through his papers, then shuffled through the papers carried by one of the 'bodyguards' had a quick whispered consultation with the man himself, and looked expectantly at the waiting prisoners.

Herbert looked round for the omnibus which was destined to carry him to work. He couldn't see one. All that he could see were four utterly decrepit clapped-out lorries. To say that they had seen better days would be a gross exaggeration. Herbert doubted if there had ever been better days, and hazarded a guess that they hailed from the time when they needed a man with a red flag to go in front of them. They would have served a better purpose if they had been melted down for scrap.

Groups One, Two and Three clambered aboard, and left. Group Four, the 'new arrivals' did not move.

"Group Four," called Brandt, excitement sharpening his voice. "Come on, Group Four. Your omnibus waits."

Group Four remained unmoving. Brandt rushed forward, and sharply slapped the side of the ancient lorry, as if it were in some way to blame. "Group Four! Your omnibus waits," he literally shrieked, his face reddening. "What is the matter?"

Silence.

The driver poked his head out of the cab, cigarette loosely hanging from the corner of his lower lip. "What the hell's going on?" he bawled. The bodyguard went over to placate him, speaking in a low undertone, while Brandt turned to face Group Four.

"What is the matter with you all?" A little drop of saliva was visible at the corner of his red little mouth.

'Frothing!" thought Herbert dourly.

"You are going to work in your omnibus! Why do you not move?"

A tall, thin chap stepped forward. "We are instructed to go to work by omnibus, so... we thought we'd wait for one to come along."

A ripple of amusement ran through the group. The Lagerführer jumped up and down. He threw his papers on the ground, and jumped on them. Never before had anyone had the audacity to question his transport arrangements. He didn't quite know how to handle this. He slapped the side of the lorry again, and it shuddered. Once more the driver stuck his head out.

"Don't do that," he bawled.

"This," screamed Brandt. "This is it. The omnibus has been provided. It is to take you to work. You are late. You must leave at once. Please get on board."

"Oh! Oh! I see!" said the tall, thin chap, as if something inexplicable had just been made clear to him. "Oh! I see! Well, you should have said, shouldn't he?" he turned around, and asked the others. "If you meant a clapped-out old lorry, you should have said so. We were waiting for a bus. Now... if you had made it clear, we could all have been at work ten minutes ago..."

At this point, the British sergeant stuck his head out of a nearby window, and sized up the situation. He grinned to himself at the sight of Brandt's discomfiture, and went back in. The new arrivals thought they had played the Lagerführer up enough for the moment. Better not overdo it on the first day, so they clambered aboard the lorry, and were rapidly driven away.

Herbert discovered that two of the prisoners in the next hut were Dutch. How on earth they had been called upon to fight in the war, he never knew. Perhaps they had volunteered, and had wanted to fight? But what really interested him was their language, and he would listen to them talking to each other for hours, without understanding a single word. Just listening to the sound of their speech. Sounds of all kinds fascinated him.

What really got him going was their singing. They would often sing, especially in the evenings, in their own language, and they had soft pleasantly untrained voices. One had a guitar and the other one a harmonica, but where they had got them, no one seemed to know. But they had them, and could play them well.

Plans were taking form in Herbert's brain. Why not another theatre project? It would give them all something to do in the evenings when they returned from work. They needed something. There were enough empty huts, and certainly enough bored prisoners. He listened spellbound to the Dutch men. They would obviously have to form the nucleus of any group, and he would have to find some way of persuading them, of winning them over to his way of thinking. At the moment, they were rather private, introspective and reserved in their dealings with the rest of the camp, keeping to themselves.

Some musical instruments would have to be obtained somehow, but he had already seen one drum kit contrived from virtually nothing, so there was no reason to suppose that this problem could not be overcome. He did a mental check of all the people in the camp and wondered what sort of pool of talent may be found. In his experience, there was always talent, if only you could 'tap' it, for the most unlikely seeming people turned out to be fairly good stand-up comics, or could play the piano like one possessed, if you could just stimulate sufficient interest to get them to have a go at it.

Returning to camp after work one evening, Herbert was delighted to see a notice pinned on to the door of the cookhouse:

A Musical Evening from Camp 31

Tonight at 8 o'clock Hut No. 1

Everyone invited

Sign... St. S Brandt.

'Great,' thought Herbert rubbing his hands. 'They must already have a group of some sort in the main camp, so we should have no trouble in getting one started here.'

At half past seven that evening, a lorry was driven into the compound and parked alongside Hut No.1. The driver hardly had time to switch off the ignition before a crowd of onlookers had gathered, and there was no shortage of volunteers to help unload. Herbert watched with mounting pleasure, for they had certainly brought the whole works along. A piano, drums, violins, accordion, guitar, trumpets, and even musical stands, a real luxury item.

The air of excitement surrounding the camp was very real, and the thought of a musical evening lifted the morale of the prisoners enormously. It had been a long time since they had heard music, and they were eager to begin. By eight o'clock the entire camp, all one hundred and thirty-seven prisoners, and six Tommies were seated in Hut No.1. (One Tommy had been left behind to 'mind the shop'.) A few had managed to bring along stools to sit on, others sat on the floor, leaned against the walls; sitting, standing or leaning, it didn't matter, they were all there.

A make-shift stage had been contrived from flat table tops, and a ten piece orchestra clambered aboard to play for Camp 31A. Herbert, leaning in a corner with Alfred, watched the performance avidly. He didn't miss a trick. And it was good, damn good. Not polished, and certainly not professional since they were all amateurs, and many of them self-taught, but the programme was well thought out, and well-rehearsed, the musicians playing well together, and a varied and good selection.

They played a few 'highbrow' pieces, as Herbert mentally termed them, including a short snatch of Wagner, but for most of the time, they played the old German songs and tunes that were familiar to all the prisoners, even from their schooldays.

Herbert began to feel again the unease of nostalgia, and a little pang of homesickness, and looking around the audience, he realised that many of them were here in flesh only, and that their hearts and thoughts were miles away, back to almost forgotten scenes and places where the music had taken them,

In the interval, whilst the orchestra had a bit of a rest, they were treated to a little comic relief in the form of a monologue and some rather vulgar jokes, the comedian wearing a bulbous red nose, and a baggy homemade suit, and the applause was deafening. Alfred felt relieved at being able to laugh at the corny jokes. He too had felt a wave of almost overwhelming homesickness, and felt that if the others had noticed, his reputation as the 'card' of the hut would be lost.

This musical evening, its undoubted success and the effect it had upon the entire camp, really settled things for Herbert. He and the Dutch men decided that they would start a small group within the camp; they would draw up some kind of draft scheme, with as many ideas as they could think up, and approach the Lagerführer.

Herbert had little or no faith in Brandt, but it was the only way of going about it. Brandt was a fool, and everyone in the camp realised this, except perhaps Brandt. Even his bodyguards tolerated him simply because they found it expedient to manipulate him, and thus got a fairly cushy berth for themselves. However, he was their first line, and approaches had to be made through him. They decided that they had better not rush at things, but wait until Brandt was in an amenable frame of mind, and not likely to be affected by a change in the moon, or any other such daft thing.

One morning, in their 'Brandt Omnibus' they set off for work, and found that they were to be engaged upon what might be a welcome change of occupation. Potato picking! Herbert had never done this before, nor had he ever given it the slightest consideration. He was a town-dweller, and as far as he was concerned, potatoes were purchased in a bag from the local greengrocer. How they actually got there never entered his calculations, and the case was the same for most other food. But they were to learn, and the hard way. Armed with buckets and sacks, they were spread out across the field, and when the potato lifter started churning them out, they were told to follow, picking up the potatoes, first into the bucket, then tip them into the sack. At first, it didn't seem so bad, quite a novelty in fact, but by the time each man reached the end of his marked out pitch, the lifter had already started down the next row, so off you had to go again, head down, and back bent double.

"Gott in Himmel!" Alfred groaned, sweating, and wiping a hand 'clawped' in mud across his moist forehead. "If that bloody lifter doesn't slow down a bit, we shall all be permanently crippled. I don't think I can straighten up now!"

Before long, the prisoners had worked out their own technique. You reached forward and picked up one potato, and, taking two steps forward, carefully placing your booted foot, you trod two or three back into the ground.

And each time you picked up potatoes, you also picked up a couple of stones to weight the sack. They got quite expert at this, but by the end of the day, even after an hour's dinner break, their backs felt as though they were about to break in half. Crawling back to their lorry and being shaken to pieces on the return journey finished most of them off, and they were to be seen helping each other back into the huts and on to the top bunks. The next day followed more or less the same pattern.

A big carthorse by the name of Dobbin (according to the farmhand who looked after him) pulled a heavy two-wheeled cart to collect the full sacks of spuds. The farmhand's name was, apparently, Joe. Whether this was his real name or not, no one ever found out, but he answered to this from all quarters. He was a tall man, standing about six and a half feet, with a long face that seemed to be drawn out, like thrown toffee. His nose lurched downwards in a hook, his chin disappeared downwards into his neck, and his jaw hung downwards in jowls. He wore an ancient blue melton coat, possessed of no buttons, loosely tied around his girth with binder twine, his overlarge feet were enshrined in size fourteen boots, and a battered flat cap perched precariously upon the extreme summit of his knobbly skull.

He said very little. In fact, he said nothing at all except two words, and these to the horse with whom he appeared to have some kind of affinity. To get the animal moving, he said "Gee-up!" and if he wanted it to stop, he said "Whoa!" and this seemed to be the limit of his conversational scope, since all the prisoner's attempts to try out their few words of English upon him failed miserably.

The men watched the performance of Joe and the horse, as they followed behind the pickers collecting the sacks. When Joe shouted "Whoa!" the horse stopped. Joe loaded the sacks on the cart, and said "Gee-up!" The patient disinterested animal then moved forward until Joe once more said "Whoa!" and as they had both done exactly this kind of thing many times before, they worked to a kind of mutual rhythm. Joe actually said "Whoa" when he had already bent down to grasp the full sack, then the cart was in just the right place for him to heave it aboard when the animal obeyed. "Gee-up", two paces or so forward, and repeat.

Alfred, head down and aching back bent, watched all this out of the corner of his eye. The rhythm was accurate and mechanical. Joe's thoughts were probably miles away, and the poor old horse was doubtless dwelling upon his forthcoming nosebag.

"Whoa!" called Joe, bending down his arms around the sack.

"Gee-up!" called Alfred, and the horse moved on.

Joe, sack half-poised, lost his rhythm and his balance, the weight of the sack dragging him forward. His size fourteens slipped on the mud, and down he went. "Whoa!" he bawled. The horse stopped, and Joe once more grasped the sack.

"Gee-up!" roared Alfred, and the cart moved off. Joe, heaving the potato sack on to where the cart should have been, found it was not there, and the sack obligingly emptied half its contents back on to the mud.

Then the rest of the prisoners joined in, and they had Joe and the poor bemused Dobbin 'Geeing-up' and Whoa-ing' all down the field. Joe began to get angry. His face reddened.

"Whoa, Dobbin! You stupid bastard!" Which was four more words than he had ever been heard to use before and then he muttered "Bloody Germans!" and "Blasted Jerries." He continued muttering that he'd be glad when knocking off time came, and was this what they had fought for, and he wasn't going to be mucked about by bloody Jerries! He didn't look to Herbert as if he had ever done much fighting, but obviously he considered that he had suffered something in the cause.

A few days later, with his back still killing him, Herbert returned to camp and found one of the Dutch men waiting for him outside his hut.

"Got a bit of bad news for you, mate," the man said. "We're being moved on tomorrow, to another camp! Don't ask me why. Why anything? We've just been told to be packed and ready to move out at eight tomorrow morning." Herbert felt distinctly put out at this.

"What about the theatre group we were going to start?" he said.

The Dutch man shrugged. "Not much I can do about it."

"Bloody hell!" Herbert swore. "What do they have to go and do this for? How many are due to go out?"

"I don't know. There's a list on the cookhouse door. There are twenty-five from our hut, but I don't know about the others."

"I suppose it's no good going to see Brandt?" Herbert asked.

"I shouldn't think so," the Dutchman said. "After all, we are still prisoners, and I suppose they can move us around if they see fit."

Herbert thought he was probably right. There was little or no point in asking Brandt anything! "We cannot help you to get your group started now," the Dutchie continued, "but the idea is a good one, and you can still use it."

Omnibus Four seemed to take longer to reach its destination the following morning, but eventually, it drew to its usual screeching halt. The guard came round to the back, and ordered seven prisoners to alight. Herbert was number six, and Alfred remained on the lorry. This was a different farm, and the farmer was leaning over the gate, obviously waiting for them. He pushed his cap to the back of his head, and said "Mornin'."

"Here y'are then," the guard said. "Seven prisoners, all hale and hearty and ready for work." He went on to make it abundantly clear that these seven prisoners were on their own, unguarded, and that they would be picked up again at four thirty, and they had better all be there, or there'd be "no end of a bloody ruckus back at the camp" and off he went.

Over the past few weeks, most of the prisoners had managed to pick up a few words of English, and frequently they actually understood more of the language than they were actually able to use. Therefore, they managed to gather, from the farmer, that their job for today was hoeing spring cabbage. He told them that one of his labourers would give them their instructions, and show them how to get on, and he gave them a hoe apiece.

They were told to hoe out the weeds, and single out each cabbage plant to two hoe's width apart. It wasn't bad work, and it was bound to be better than potato picking. As they moved down the field, the cleaned rows looked quite impressive, and Herbert found that he rather liked this job. It was tidy and orderly, and it fitted in with his scheme of things. He didn't like cabbage plants just growing all over the place, willy-nilly. With the German passion for neatness, it delighted him to instruct the cabbage where it should grow, to line it up with its neighbour, and to remove all intruding weeds. If he had been able to do so, he would have liked to ensure that all the rows were dead straight with the use of long pieces of string, and to have checked that all the plants grew at exactly the same rate so that they were all of uniform height!

The mid-day ration had been supplied by the camp kitchen, as usual, and a quarter pound of tea had been included for a brew up. By the use of sign language, and the few English words they knew, they persuaded the farm labourer to get the farmer's wife to make them a brew of tea. They hoped that, since it was on a farm, she might put some fresh milk in it, and perhaps a little sugar. Sweet, milky tea! Just what they could do with! But when it arrived, it was black! Black as soot, and not unlike that in substance and smell! The whole ration had been used to brew about a pint of tea, and it was totally undrinkable. Herbert smelled it, and tasted a little on the end of his finger. He spat it out. 'My God,' he thought. 'You'd need to change your socks if you drank any of that. The housefrau must be very anti-German.'

The prisoners ate the rations that had been provided for them with their usual sharp appetites, but nobody wanted the tea. They threw it under the hedge, and a dandelion visibly wilted with a cry of pain.

That evening, back in his hut, Herbert received a summons to the presence of Staff Sergeant Brandt. It was issued more in the nature of a command, and Herbert's first reaction was to say 'Get stuffed', but then he decided he had better go and see what the hell Brandt wanted. Daft little bugger! Brandt was inclined to be benevolent.

"Ah! Baum-Hacker," he said, allowing a smile to hover around his pinched red little mouth.

"You are to have a visitor this evening, from the main camp. The interpreter, English of course, has been in touch with me today, and he is coming to have a chat with you."

"Any idea what it's about? Staff?" asked Herbert.

"No! He didn't say, and I thought it advisable not to enquire too closely." 'That figures,' Herbert thought. "It sounds as if it might be trouble, and you wouldn't want to know! It might upset your comfortable little set up!"

Walking back to the hut to get cleaned up, Herbert felt vaguely apprehensive. He did a quick mental flash back of all the things he and Alfred had done, and said. Or had not done, and left unsaid, but could find nothing to account for this visit.

"I'm going to be grilled by MI5," he told Alfred.

"Some people have all the luck. Nobody bothers to grill me, I'm not that important," Alfred said, grinning.

Herbert was again summoned to Brandt's office later that evening, and found an English staff sergeant lounging against the desk, quite at ease, and smoking.

"This is Baum-Hacker," Brandt said.

"Cigarette?" said the visitor, handing the packet in Herbert's direction.

"Nein! Thank you, I don't smoke." Herbert was a little disconcerted to hear such good German from the Englishman. Colloquial, and with a good accent too!

"I have been sent to ask you a few questions!"

"Here goes," Herbert muttered silently. 'Now they have found out that I shouldn't be here at all. That they sent me to the wrong camp, and they're going to move me on again. Bugger it!'

The staff sergeant continued.

"When prisoners get moved on from camp to camp, we nearly always receive a file on them, in due course. And looking through your file, it has been noticed that you were connected with an amateur theatre group in your last camp, Camp 29. Were an enthusiastic member, in fact. Is this correct?"

Herbert nodded.

"Good! Well that's okay then. Now! We have a theatre group in Camp 31, which is very badly in need of new life, new talent, and a few new ideas. We need to keep you chaps in better spirits, at least until you are all able to be shipped back home. What I want to do is to take you from here, and transfer you to the main camp, so that you can take charge of the theatre group. All right?"

Herbert was utterly dumbfounded. Here he had been expecting trouble, expecting all kinds of things, and all they wanted him for was some more play acting. They were an unpredictable lot, the British. "When do I have to go?" he asked.

"Oh! Now. At once. I'm going to take you back with me. That's okay, isn't it?" Herbert mutely nodded. "Right! Then go and pack your kit-bag, and report back here in ten minutes."

Alfred was waiting for him back at the hut.

"What happened?"

"You're not going to believe this." Herbert was not sure he believed it himself. "They want me for the theatre group in Camp 31. I'm to take charge, and they are transferring me especially. Now! Tonight! I've got to be ready in ten minutes!"

Alfred's customary grin left his face. "Oh! Sod it!" he said. There was a moment of silence between them.

"We've got along fine haven't we?" Alfred continued. "I shall bloody well miss you."

Herbert thumped him on the back. "Don't you worry, old mate. You won't have time to miss me. Just let me get over there, and get started, and then I shall say that I need a carpenter experienced in stage work, and I shall ask if they can transfer you!"

Between them, they managed to get all Herbert's things stuffed into his kit-bag in double quick time, and with a brief handshake, and 'Cheerio' all round, he set off at a run, back to Brandt's office.

Standing outside, with a lumpy kit-bag by his side, and still breathing heavily, he could hardly believe it. He hoped it was all right, and not some kind of trick. It seemed a little odd to him that the British should be concerning themselves with the morale of German POWs in their hands, but he supposed that they thought they were easier to handle, easier to get work out of, if they were in good spirits. He really wanted to get into this theatre group. Really wanted it.

Of course, what he really wanted to do, just like everybody else, was to go home, and make a fresh start, but he pushed this thought to the back of his mind. They would all be sent home, and perhaps in the not too distant future. But... meantime, there was time to be got through, and life to be lived the best way he could. For him, the theatre group was his life-line, his safety valve. Without this, or something very akin to it, he occasionally doubted if he would make it.

The officer appeared from the doorway of Brandt's office, and motioned him into the waiting truck. As they drove off into the night, Herbert thought about Alfred. He would miss him. They were on the same wavelength, he and Alfred. Captivity meant living a bit closer to one's fellow men than one would otherwise be able to do, or even want to do. He and Alfred made a good team, and it was not going to end now, if he could help it. Just give him a day or two to find his feet, to get the lie of the land. He would get Alfred transferred to help with the theatre thing. He'd have to, if he could. And he'd really need him anyway. Pity to break up now when the end seemed almost in sight... No! Just a few days, and he would do something about Alfred...

CHAPTER VII:

Camp 31, Warwickshire

The tyres of the truck whooshed on the wet surface of the road as it drew to a halt before the gates of the main camp. Herbert reflected, gloomily, that whenever he was in transit, it always seemed to be raining. The big lamp glowed over the gate, and the rain made iridescent rays of light around it. Behind, the camp was a mere series of indefinable shapes against the night sky.

The guardroom door opened, and a sentry carrying a meagre torch peered into the truck. Once again, Herbert's hurriedly packed kit-bag was emptied onto the guardroom floor, and the half-asleep sentry picked over his belongings. Apparently satisfied that he had done his duty, he said, "You'll have to spend the night in here. We'll give you a cell, just for the one night, and in the morning you can report to your Lagerführer."

'Blimey! A cell!' Herbert thought, and for a second, felt a bit like a criminal. He wondered if they would lock him in, and hoped that they wouldn't. He didn't relish the thought of being locked into a small confined space, but they didn't.

The sentry tossed him three blankets, and told him he would have to make do for the one night. Herbert thought he could make do very well, and lying down he made himself as comfortable as a seasoned campaigner and veteran prisoner can. He relaxed, and allowed his mind to dwell upon the possibilities; what would he be allowed to do for the theatre group; could he get really ambitious, or were the facilities as limited as they had been in the other camp?

He felt a flicker of panic when he realised that he knew no one at all in this camp, that he had been brought here all on his own, and he would have to start all over again, getting to know people, making friends, fitting in. Ah well! He'd worry about that tomorrow, he'd sort it out all right. He had managed thus far... and he fell asleep.

"You will be shot at daybreak," the officer shouted. Herbert began to shake, and the sweat burst out upon his forehead. He was back on the Russian front, and fighting. The shell fire was continuous, and the bright flashes illuminated the softly falling snow. It was all for the Glory of the Vaderland, and the Third Reich. And the Führer too. There was his wireless truck, and he had been sent to repair the telephone link from headquarters to No.4 Battery.

Gunter Wesel, the driver, and Herbert's mate, was getting damned cheesed off with all these bloody repair jobs, he said. As soon as they reinstated one line of communication, another one went. Every time Herbert reached out with his hand, for the broken wire, a Russian soldier slapped him on the back.

"Do not touch it comrade," he threatened. Herbert moved in a fog of bewilderment. He had a sensation of being weightless, of floating above the ground, of hovering outside his own body.

Who was that standing over there? What on earth was his old schoolmaster doing, carrying a large cardboard box, and walking through the firing, the front line fighting? He tried to call out to him, to tell him to look out but no sound came from his lips. He could not move, his feet were frozen to the ground.

Alfred appeared in the distance, walking slowly, swaying from side to side, and for some reason he was carrying a red overcoat, the colour of blood, across his arm. Herbert watched his approach, but could not move towards him, nor attract his attention. Alfred passed by him so closely that their arms brushed, but Alfred did not see him, for on his face was a look of horror, and Alfred was completely bald. In place of the shock of curly blonde

134

hair, was a gleaming white pate. Alfred soundlessly, unseeingly disappeared in the distance.

Herbert saw a tree, and something propped up against it. It was his old bicycle, the one he used to pedal to school on, and from the saddlebag, there came a faint cry. He moved nearer, lifting his feet slowly, as if they were leaden, and he tried to force open the saddlebag, but it was secured with an enormous padlock. He attacked it desperately, and wrenched at it, but it would not budge. He tore at the worn leather, sobbing, until his nails were broken, but it would not move. The crying continued, and sounded like that of a small child. He had to do something, he had to get it out of that saddlebag, he must break the padlock.

He looked up, and there was the same Russian officer. Herbert recognised the face, for he had seen the man lying dead and frozen in the snow, the flesh blue tinged.

"You will be shot at daybreak," the face said, grinning, and Herbert noticed that the teeth were brown and broken. "You will be shot at daybreak," the man repeated, in a toneless sing-song voice. And Herbert passed out. He felt himself hit the ground, and the impact awakened him. He opened his eyes, and he was still bathed in the sweat of fear.

For a moment, he could not remember where he was, and then he realised what had happened. He had fallen off the narrow shelf bed in the cell, and hit the ground.

"For Christ's sake, pull yourself together Herbert," he said sternly, but the dream was still very real. He climbed back among the blankets for the rest of the night, but the feeling of fear and apprehension remained with him.

He was eventually wakened by the clanging sound as the sentry dropped a bucket outside the cell door, and stretching, yawning and scratching, he forced himself to face reality. Half an hour later, he stood before the Lagerführer of Camp 31.

'Thank God he isn't another daft bugger like Brandt,' was Herbert's first reaction. This man seemed a decent sort, middle height, middle-aged and slightly balding, with the air of one determined to do his best against overwhelming odds. His attitude was kindly, even painstaking.

"I'm sure you will be alright here," he told Herbert. "You will go to work, of course," the officer continued. "Then, in your spare time, you can start re-organising the theatre business. We have had some shows, and some quite good ones, but some of our best chaps have been moved on, and now we are down to rock bottom. So... you'll just have to do your best."

"I will do what I can, Chief," Herbert promised, and meant it. "I'm rather keen on this sort of thing."

"I will naturally do all that I can to help," said the Lagerführer. "Meanwhile, there is a spare bed in Hut 19. Go and see the orderly and get yourself settled in. He'll put you right on everything."

Herbert swung his kit-bag on to his shoulder, and set off to find Hut 19 and the Hut orderly.

A middle-aged fellow was sweeping out the hut when Herbert eventually found it, giving it apparently its daily 'do round'. He was stooped, with a sallow skin, and watery blue eyes, and he handled the broom as if it weighed a ton. He seemed only too glad of a reason to stop, when he saw Herbert coming towards him.

"Is there a spare bunk in here? Which one?"

"You the new chap from 31A?"

"Yes! Baum-Hacker!"

"Klaus Meister!" And they shook hands.

Herbert told him about having to spend the previous night in the cell in the guardroom, and in return Meister gave him the run down on the camp, in some detail. He told him what to do, and what to be careful not to do, what to look out for, and Herbert listened with only one ear. He'd find most of this out for himself, later. He allowed Meister to ramble on, while he unpacked his few things.

Everybody else at the camp had by this time been taken out to work, and tomorrow Herbert would be out at work too, but for today, he could have a walk around, look the camp over, make a mental survey.

He found a barber shop, a canteen, a church, a sick-bay (with a dentist), and a washroom, with showers. There was a tailor's shop, a cobblers, cookhouse, and, last of all, opposite to the main gate, the theatre. "My God!" He was truly amazed at the scope of the camp, and thought the only thing that had not been thoughtfully provided was a brothel.

He reflected that his native good luck had not deserted him after all, especially since he was supposed to have been sent to a Nazi Camp to be politically converted.

He found the small door at the rear of the theatre unlocked, and went inside. The smell was familiar, and to Herbert, exciting. The smell was of greasepaint, of paint, wood shavings, dust, and chalk. Once again, in his fantasy world, his spirits lifted. He stood in the wings, and let the atmosphere eddy around him.

He wandered on to the centre stage, smiling to himself, and for a blissful moment, he fancied he could hear the echo of past applause, as he looked out over the auditorium. He was no longer a prisoner of war; he forgot he was liable to orders, to be told what to do and where to go. He was a performer, an artiste, a musician. He held the centre of the stage, and in his head, he heard the sound of a ghostly orchestra.

The auditorium was filled with bench seats sloping slightly towards the stage, and there was even an orchestra pit. The place had everything; what more could any amateur ask? The scope was enormous, Herbert felt. They could put on all kinds of shows here, music, revues, concerts, straight plays. Have a go at the classics? Or just write things for themselves? Anything. As he stood there, his thoughts chasing each other around in his brain, and the little man inside his head jumping up and down with glee, he felt his temporary fears evaporate. He'd do alright here, and he could hardly wait to get started.

As he reluctantly turned to leave the stage, he became aware of being watched. A thin undersized little chap, his prisoner's uniform hanging loosely on his narrow shoulders, gazed morosely up at him from the direction of the orchestra pit.

"You looking for something?" he asked.

"No, not really! Just having a look around," replied Herbert.

"You must be new here, I haven't seen you before!"

"I've just been transferred here from 31A," Herbert went on to explain. "I've been told that I'm here to help with the theatre group... that's why I came to look at the theatre."

The light chap brightened up. "That's great, mate. I'm damn glad about that. We've had a few things here, you know. But some of the good ones have been sent on, and it needs a bit of pepping up, or something." He sat down on the wooden steps, and fishing out a nub end from some inner depth of his clothing, lighted up. "You smoke, mate?"

Herbert shook his head, and there was a companiable sort of silence between them.

"Fact is," the little chap went on, "now that the bloody war is over, they've only got one thing on their minds most of them. When can they go home?"

"We should all like to know the answer to that one," Herbert said with some feeling.

"Yes, of course. And it's understandable, I suppose. Especially if you've got something to go back home to," the other man said, and he sounded wistful. Herbert thought it better not to enquire whether he had something to go back to, or not. He finished his smoke with a last deep pull, and ground the shred of cigarette end beneath the heel of his boot. "The way I see it," he said, looking Herbert straight in the face, "is that it's all going to take time. Red tape, papers, documents, and all that sort of thing. So, we might as well do something to make the time pass quicker."

"You're too damn right," Herbert said with real feeling.

"I'm the general dogsbody around here. They call me Spreit. It's Springer, really, but I'm known as Spreit throughout the camp. Information, fetching, carrying, organising, getting something mended... You name it, I'll do it!" A note of personal pride crept into the little man's voice, and his meagre chest seemed to swell slightly.

"Thanks! I'll remember that," Herbert answered, and then, with a change of tone, "What's the rest of the theatre group like, the ones that are left here?"

"Oh! Great! They're a good bunch, and they work well together. Heinemann, the band leader, runs it at the moment, but he is really only interested in the music side. He's very good mind, but not a great one for ideas! You know, music all the time. I like the music, mind you, but... well, I like a good laugh, or a bit of a sketch or something..."

Herbert met the theatre group that night, and it seemed to him that there were enough people interested to get together a reasonable show. The main trouble seemed to be that there were a great many people who were willing, even anxious, to do the work behind the scenes, but not enough willing to actually go on stage.

Herbert regaled them with stories of his theatrical experiences as an amateur, before the war, slightly exaggerated, of course, and Heinemann was obviously impressed, as Herbert had intended he should be. In fact, he seemed to be rather relieved to be able to hand over some of the responsibilities to someone else. The sense of being a newcomer, even perhaps an intruder, left him, and when the group split up to return to their individual huts that night, Herbert had already promised to work out some reasonable suggestions, and to have them ready the next time they met.

Walking back across the darkened compound to Hut 19, Herbert felt good. He had the theatre, his own private fantasy world in which he could be almost anything he chose, he had met 'his' group and they seemed all right. Reasonable, likeable. And they had not resented him. They might well have felt that they didn't want to be organised, and were quite happy as they were. Passive non-cooperation on their part would have made things very difficult. But, he reflected with a slight degree of complacency, he need not have worried.

Herbert was a fairly easy chap to get on with. Undemanding, not given to moods, or if he was, he kept them very well hidden. Most days found him with the same even temper. He had few irritating habits, and he could chat, or be quiet, as the occasion arose. It therefore followed that he had no difficulty in making friends, and even those who were not his particular cronies, always had a friendly word, and in a very short time, he had quite settled down to the routine of his new camp.

This camp had previously been occupied by Italian prisoners, but they had all now left, and were working on farms around and about, and living in. What really surprised Herbert was that the camp was guarded by German POWs, except for the guardroom by the main gate, which was commanded by the British.

Prisoners worked in the kitchen, stores, canteen, and wherever there was work to be done. Halfway up the drive was the lorry park, and the labour office, which was again manned by the prisoners themselves. True, there was one civilian, a man from the Ministry of Agriculture, who was supposed to be in charge, but he seemed to be totally disenchanted with the whole thing, and in Herbert's opinion, was unlikely to be able to organise even a booze-up in a brewery.

And the prisoners were excellent at organising themselves, so... he left it all to them. Just so long as someone brought him a cup of tea at fairly frequent intervals, a packet of Woodbines, and the daily newspaper, he was quite happy, and gave no trouble.

One or two Tommies did still accompany the lorries taking the prisoners outside to their work, but this was more for the look of the thing than any actual intention to prevent them from taking off. If they had really wanted to, a lorry load of prisoners could have overpowered the guard and the driver, and driven the lorry off, but... where to?

Herbert was one of a party of some fifteen prisoners, leaving the main gate for their daily work stint. After about a mile, the vehicle screeched to a halt, and Herbert wondered if they ever slowed down. They never seemed to. It seemed as if they were always driven flat out, and then at the last minute there was a slam on the brakes, and a screech of tyres on the road.

"We there already?" he asked.

Pete Scholer, sitting next to him, smiled tolerantly. "No, mate! This is our normal routine stop," and a grin split his face right across. He went on, "We have an arrangement with our guard. This little chap is the only one responsible for us, and our return to camp. He is terrified that one of these days, we will have cleared off, and he will be on the carpet back at camp. So, he supplies us daily with cigarettes, and in return for the fags, he expects us to behave, and give him our word that we'll make no trouble. That's where he is at the moment. Gone shopping for our fags." They all laughed.

"Poor little sod," another said. "Where on earth does he think we should run to?"

Just then the guard returned with forty Woodbines, which he handed into the lorry with a faintly apologetic air. These were evenly distributed among the prisoners, and when Herbert tried to refuse his share on the grounds that he did not smoke, Pete Scholer told him not to be so bloody daft.

"Keep them," he said, "and use them for trading. It's surprising what you can get with a few fags."

So Herbert put them in his pocket, and the lorry moved on, not stopping again until they arrived at the farm where they were to work on ditching again.

Later on in the week, the working party had changed, and Herbert and five other prisoners were sent to help with threshing. This was something new, and none of them had ever done it before, nor had they seen it being done.

When they arrived at the farm on their first day, one surprise awaited them. Standing near the Dutch barn were three girls.

"Look at that," Klaus Bremer nudged Herbert. "Women. Real live ones, at that!" The girls, realising that all eyes were turned upon them, reddened slightly. The prisoners made ribald comments to each other in German, confident that the girls would not understand.

Klaus Bremer said they must be the Women's Land Army, for they wore dark brown breeches, and khaki coloured shirts, and he said he had heard about them. They were called up, like being called up into the forces, but they were to work on the land, and taking the place of men who had been conscripted into the army. The girls seemed ordinary enough, and quite pleasant, but it had been a very long time since the prisoners had encountered female company of any kind, and perforce, they had to swagger a little.

After a lot of coughing and spluttering, the tractor was eventually started, and a long jumping, twisted belt, flapping wildly, got the threshing box going. A cloud of dust immediately enveloped the whole operation. Herbert and another chap were told to go to the top of the corn rick, and pitch the sheaves on to the threshing box, where a waiting farm labourer was to feed them into the drum.

All the work seemed to be dirty work, but the three girls were given the muckiest of the lot. They had to gather the chaff into a big sheet, carry it into the barn, up a ladder and into the loft. Two of the girls were quite substantial and robust-looking, with smooth skinned arms, and a faintly suntanned complexion. Sturdy, peasant stock,

142

Herbert mentally classified them, but the third was a little thin thing, no bigger than a two penny stamp. She was a wispy, washed out pale blonde, with scared blue eyes, and narrow bones. 'Town bred,' thought Herbert again. She was visibly wilting under the strain, and seemed to have great difficulty in keeping up the pace of the rest. Twice disaster almost overcame her when, halfway up the ladder, the weight of the laden sheet proved more than she could manage, and down she came.

When this happened for the second time, Albert Schmidt who had been watching from the corner of his eye was overcome with compunction. The work was too heavy for her, he thought.

It was not work for a woman, and she was only a little bit of a thing. It was a shame! And she seemed so distressed, that he thought he would help her, be chivalrous, play the 'gallant'. He would offer to do her job, and she could perhaps do his.

He walked over to her, talking in German, of which she understood not a word. He caught hold of the offending sheet, and pointed. He mimed that he would do this for her, and he made circles with his hands. The girl was too terrified to try to understand, or perhaps too thick. She drew back from Albert, and he, in his anxiety to make her understand that he merely wanted to be helpful, followed her and caught hold of her hand.

As soon as he touched her, she let out a piercing scream. Albert spoke soothingly. She screamed again, and he dropped her hand. She continued screaming, almost hysterical, and tears gushed from her pale little eyes making streaks in the dust on her cheeks. Albert spoke to her as one would to a child, but again in German which she did not understand. The farmer came running from the house, and Albert walked towards him, trying to explain. The farmer was not interested.

"Leave those girls alone, you bloody Jerries," he roared. "Get back to your work."

Poor old Albert tried again. He certainly deserved an 'A' for effort.

"You've got it all wrong," he said, in German, but the farmer didn't understand either. The rest of the prisoners gathered around, and tried to help, but none of them had more than a few odd words of English, and they all talked at once, this only made matters worse.

The farmer was red with anger. "Shut up! And get back to bloody work!" he roared. "What do you think you are here for?" And he strode off back towards the house.

The silly girl was still sobbing, and being patted on the shoulder by the other two. Albert looked around him helplessly, and shrugged his shoulders. All he had wanted was to be helpful, and what a furore he had started. He gave it up, and returned to his appointed job.

Ten minutes later, a truck drew up in the farmyard, with the usual screech of brakes applied at the last minute, and two men alighted. The farmer emerged from the house, and joined them, and altogether they walked towards the unfortunate Albert, who was promptly seized by each arm, bundled into the truck and rapidly driven away. Apparently the farmer had telephoned the camp, made a complaint against Albert, and requested his immediate removal as a troublemaker. Poor old Albert, totally misunderstood, had to spend twenty-one days in the 'cooler'.

Herbert had never heard of basic slag. He didn't even know what it was, but he was to come to know it very well, and in fact one might say intimately. He had to work with it all day long, spreading it over the fields, and it was foul muck. It got into the pores of the skin and mixed freely with the sweat of honest toil; it caked in the hair, and encrusted eyebrows and lashes, it got into the eyes and settled firmly into the inner corners, mingling with the natural moisture to form uncomfortable lumps.

After a relatively short time, the only thing any of them could think of was hot water. Hot water to shower, to fill a deep tub to sit in, to wash hair and clothing, steaming hot water to open up the pores and remove the ingrained filth of the slag.

And the hot water at the camp was, to put it mildly, temperamental. It hardly ever worked properly during the week, and not often at weekends. Therefore, when it did show itself, just for a change, the word rapidly spread around, and everybody rushed to use it, to perform delayed ablutions, and laundry. Those who got there had it at best, and the remainder lost out. By the end of a day or two of basic slag, Herbert had 'lost out' and looked like nothing so much as a chimney sweep, as indeed did most of the others on the same job, with just the middle of their faces roughly washed with cold water.

Four of them were working on this job at Elm Farm for the last four days. Sack after sack of the filthy stuff had been spread over the fields with the aid of a mechanical spreader, and on the Friday morning, after only half an hour, they could already taste it, and their eyes, noses and throats were full. The spreader broke down in the top field.

"Bugger the bloody thing, it's wore out, the driver swore with feeling sprung out of intimate acquaintance. The old man 'ull play 'ell about this!" the farmer exclaimed.

Herbert and the others were standing aside, mopping at their faces with bits of rag, and telling each other what a bloody filthy job this was, when the farmer drove up. He was a man with an air of authority, of middle years, and he wore a 'good' tweed jacket, breeches, boots and gaiters. "What's up, Jim? Why have you stopped?" he said to the farmhand. "Spreader's bust, sir! I think it's wore out!"

"Damn and blast! That's all we need, and we're behind already. It's bound to need some new part that nobody can get hold of, and there'll be weeks of delay." He rubbed his chin thoughtfully, and had a quick look at the offending machine.

"Well, the bloody job's got to be done! They'll have to do it by hand. Put the bags on the trailer and drive round the field that way." And he went into closer consultation with him.

Ernst Eichmann caught some of the conversation. He had picked up a few words of English, and gathered the basis of what the farmer had said. He looked wrathful.

"What's he on about?" Herbert asked him.

"He wants us to sit on the back of a trailer and spread this bloody filthy stuff by hand, that's all. The stupid bugger can do the bleeding job himself! I've just about had enough of basic slag, and of the Tommies! And of dirty work."

The farmer turned around when Ernst began to speak, and putting his hands casually into his pockets, he strolled over to him. Then, in fluent German: "Oh! So you've had enough of Tommies, and dirty work, have you?" he said. "You think I should do the bloody job myself, do you? And if I did, what the hell use would you be here then? Perhaps you should have thought of all this before you joined?" He paused, and then added in a lower tone, "I could report you to the commandant, you know. But, of course, I won't. Now if you have finished letting off steam, let's get on with the job, shall we? Enough time has been wasted." He grinned sardonically at the discomfited Eichmann, and left.

Eichmann was utterly confounded, and the other prisoners laughed. They had all taken it for granted, wherever they had been working, that they could converse freely among themselves, and be fairly sure that no one else would understand what they said. Their comments upon persons and places were frequently both pointed and vulgar, and it rather tickled them that they could get away with it.

Eichmann reddened, and had the grace to look sheepish. Here he was, in the middle of England, and out of the blue, an English farmer who looked as if he didn't know 'A' from a Bull's Foot' had told him off in no uncertain terms, speaking his own language perfectly, and if the truth be told, with a much better accent than Eichmann himself.

"Near one that?" Herbert chuckled, nudging Eichmann. "You could have ended up with old Albert."

"You can't win 'em all," said Eichmann. "Basic slag he wants, and basic slag he'll bloody well get..." And the wind blew stronger for good measure.

Back at the camp preparations for a performance at the theatre were in full swing. Herbert had put forward his suggestions, and they had eventually decided upon a light variety programme for the first half of the evening, incorporating some musical solos, a few card tricks by Gunter Wesel in which the audience were invited to 'pick a card, any card' and which often turned out badly. In fact, if he got seven out of ten, he was doing well, but the audience thought that this was all part of the act, and Wesel shaped up his patter accordingly.

Albert Schmidt, released from the 'cooler', was to sing, in a rather nasal tenor voice, some stirring German songs which would undoubtedly cause waves of nostalgia to flow through the assembled prisoners, and this would be followed by a stand-up comic who, wearing a false red nose, and flapping soled overlarge boots, would tell some dreadful corny jokes that he was already collecting. The second half of the evening was to consist of a one-act play, written by some of the lads, and containing some pithy comments upon farmers, versus prisoners of war working for them.

Rehearsals were going well, and the only snag they had so far encountered was the part of the farmer's wife in the play. It was necessary that she should be young and attractive, because in the final scene, the prisoner and the wife ended up in bed together, and were caught out by the irate husband. Female clothing was desperately needed and obviously there was none readily available. One of the chaps on an outside working party happened, by the merest chance he said, to espy a line of washing, and as if by magic, dress, stockings, knickers (of a suitable frilly variety) brassiere and nightdress, all found their way beneath his tunic, and stuffed down the legs of his working trousers, from whence they were produced at rehearsal, and no questions asked.

A blonde wig was contrived from lengths of binder twine, each prisoner purloining a few bits from whichever farm he happened to be working on at the moment. This was dressed by the camp barber and behold, the complete glamorous farmer's wife.

The actual part was given to Werner Gunn, because he had rather a young, even a 'girlish' face. It was necessary, however, to shave off some of his eyebrows which were considerably bushier than those of the average farmer's wife, and although he protested volubly, and refused to listen to reason, they sat on his chest, and did it anyway. While they were at it, they shaved his legs which were covered in dark wiry hair.

By the time they had made him up, dressed him in the stolen clothes, and stuffed his bra with rolled-up socks to give him a rather improbable shape, he began to look quite attractive! When they told him this, he warned them not to try anything, unless they wanted their faces bashed in! Once he had got his costume, he entered into the part with gusto, and practised walking, swinging his hips and buttocks in what he fondly imagined must be a 'feminine' fashion, although Herbert privately thought it looked more like 'duck'd disease'.

The night of the performance arrived, and a few of the British officers who had accepted invitations were seated in the audience. It was obviously going well, judging by the great guffaws and belly laughs. Schmidt's singing was loudly applauded, and even the comic's jokes, most of which they must have heard before, went down well. Gunter Wesel got his seven out of ten, and even invited the British commandant to 'pick a card, any card...'

After the interval came the play and this was an enormous and unqualified success. Although the British contingent did not understand it all, they got the message.

148

They must have done, for the farmer was portrayed as a total straw in the mouth clod, with a gay young wife, bored and unsatisfied with her elderly husband, and who welcomed the advances of the handsome, gallant, heroic German prisoner!

The handsome prisoner would then be asked to stay and 'help her in the house' while the doltish farmer went out and spread his own basic slag! The nuances and overtones were much appreciated by the prisoners, who absolutely roared, whilst the British, not fully understanding the implications and the ramifications of the German language, laughed politely, but with the mental reservation that the Germans were easily amused.

The play was the sole topic of conversation around the camp for days following, and already Herbert was constantly being asked to do another one 'with a woman in it'. Poor Werner Gunn! It looked as if he might almost be typecast! Herbert was honestly overjoyed with his first effort, and with the way the theatre group had all pulled around and worked together. The prisoner's appreciation was genuine; he basked in the limelight, and his head was full of ambitious ideas.

The group was fortunate in that they had a good carpenter, who worked away quietly in the background, and managed to produce the scenery and props required. His ingenuity was little short of miraculous, but there was one drawback. He was meticulous, and thus a little on the slow side. He refused to be hurried, he was a craftsman, and he cared nothing for the 'showbiz' hurly-burly. He would do the job properly, or not at all, and they would just have to wait. Herbert noted all this, and thought perhaps the time was now ripe to try and get his old pal Alfred transferred as he had promised to do.

He had thought a great deal about Alfred, and indeed he had missed him, but he had not wanted to rush his fences, and he had certainly not wanted to upset anybody, and spoil the whole thing, just when he had got it going.

He thought he would have a quick word with the Lagerführer, or perhaps Staff Schneider. He was in and around the camp fairly often, and as luck would have it, Herbert ran into him crossing the compound on the very day he had made up his mind to have a word with him. They had a fairly length conversation about the theatre group, and how it might be shaping up. Schneider had thoroughly enjoyed the performance, he said, and was still chuckling over the performance of Werner Gunn as the farmer's wife. This seemed propitious time to mention Alfred, and Schneider said he would see what he could do, but obviously he could promise nothing.

Three days later, a familiar figure, mop of hair standing out all round his head, his face almost split in two with the wideness of his grin, walked through the main gate of the camp, and enquired for Herbert. They thumped each other enthusiastically on the back, and muttered, 'Good Old Schneider'.

Herbert was rather glad that he had saved all his previously unwanted cigarettes that Pete Scholer had urged him to accept, for with a bit of bribery here, and a promise or two there, he and Alfred were once again in the same hut.

Alfred settled down into the life of Camp 31 as if he had never been anywhere else, and he immediately got on the right side of the theatre carpenter by saying that he hoped he would allow him to be a bit of help, since he hoped to learn something from him. He wanted to go back to the trade when he returned home to Germany, and this, of course delighted the older man, who was only too anxious to play the game of teacher and pupil. Herbert had not known that Alfred could be so diplomatic!

CHAPTER VIII

Herbert, Alfred and a chap called Fritz were the small working party sent out to an unfamiliar farm, ostensibly to muck out the farmyard. The lorry dropped them at the end of the long drive, and clutching their issue of mid-day rations, they headed towards the house, where the farmer greeted them in a friendly fashion, and showed them what was required of them. The yard was thick with manure that had obviously been there for a very long time.

"Some right good stuff," Fritz said, thinking back to the time when he had been rather keen on gardening at home.

They got stuck into the work with a will, and before long the farmer came from the house carrying a tall brown jug of piping hot tea, and three mugs. The prisoners looked at each other, and then at him! They didn't usually get given anything. They took a short break, downed the tea, and were profuse in their thanks.

Alfred then had what he considered later to be one of his more brilliant ideas. He offered to return the jug and the mugs to the farmhouse, and whilst he was there, he would ask the farmer's wife if she would prepare their mid-day ration for them. His knowledge of English was slight, but he was determined to have a go at it.

He knocked politely on what he took to be the kitchen door of the farmhouse, and a pleasant looking woman opened it. 'Now!' he thought nervously, and remembering what Herbert had told him about Albert Schmidt. 'I must not frighten her!' He smiled, bowed slightly, and held towards her the rations they had brought with them. There were three half rashers of bacon, a knob of margarine, half a loaf of bread, and three small sausages. She looked at them in Alfred's none too clean hands. "Yes?" she said.

Alfred cleared his throat, and launched into the speech he had been preparing. "Please?" he said. "You cook? Mine friends and ich. This, ja? From camp we bring!"

The woman shook her head uncomprehendingly. "You want what?" But her tone was kindly, and Alfred, blushing slightly, took heart and tried again.

"Please? You cook. Mine friends and ich. From camp, ja?"

Enlightenment dawned, and the woman smiled. "Oh! I see! This is your dinner, and you would like me to fry it for you?"

"Ja! Please! Thank you," Alfred struggled with the unfamiliar sounds, and placed the precious rations in her hands.

"Is this all they give you?"

"Please?" asked Alfred.

"Yes, alright. I'll be glad to fry it for you, but is this all?"

"Ja, all!" and Alfred, bowing slightly again, turned and fled back to the farmyard. He was rather pleased with himself, and boasted a bit when he joined the other two. He had had his first conversation in a foreign language, with an English woman, and he felt he had done rather well!

The three of them slogged away for the rest of the morning, with no tricks and no slacking. The work was hard, and dirty, but they felt obliged to do their best, if only to show their gratitude for the jug of tea, and the farmer's friendly attitude.

About dinner time, the farmer reappeared from the direction of the house, carrying a tray with three plates.

"Grub's up!" he shouted. "Come on," and motioned them towards a wooden summer house. "You can eat in here, alright?" and he laid out the three plates on the table. They stared in disbelief, for the large plates were full, almost overflowing, with bacon, liver, eggs, potatoes and fried bread. It was a meal of a kind they had not seen in a long time. Although the food at the camp was adequate, and they were not now so constantly hungry as they had been at first, nevertheless, they were hungry for taste and flavour rather than quantity.

They all began to speak at once, to say some kind of thanks to the farmer, who stood grinning at them.

"Can't understand your lingo, boys," he said, and waved his hand deprecatingly. "Hope you enjoy it!" and he went back to the house, presumably to enjoy his own.

Sitting down in deck chairs, they gazed at the food with reverence, and then with a whoop, they picked up the knives and forks and dived in. They ate silently, and when at last Fritz had mopped his plate clean with the last crumb of his bread, a slight belch as he leaned back in the chair, broke the quiet. He sought with his tongue among his back teeth for a crumb of liver that had lodged there. Then he said, grinning, "I don't reckon my sausage was among that lot, but - I'm not complaining!"

There was a different job lined up for them in the afternoon. They were to help the farmer castrate some eight or so young bulls. Bullocks, he called them. Herbert thought he hadn't heard all right!

"Ballocks?" he asked. The farmer grinned.

"No! Not ballocks! Bullocks! Bullocks! Boy cows? You understand?" Herbert shook his head, and shrugged.

"Bullocks? Boy cows? No! Okay?"

All four of them went round to where the animals were already standing in a special pen, and Herbert and Alfred were told to catch them, one by one, and lead them to the railings. It soon became obvious to Herbert that the bullocks were definitely anti-German, but eventually they managed to get hold of the first one, with Herbert hanging on to the beast's tail, and Alfred with two fingers stuck up its nostrils. They hung a rope around its neck, and made it fast to the railings.

The farmer squatted behind the animal, and with a razor sharp knife, he slit open the scrotum and two pink testicles popped out. A pair of pincers separated them, and Fritz, standing by with a bucket of cold water, and trying to look in the opposite direction, heard them plop into it. Some kind of antiseptic was dabbed on to the empty bag, and the farmer called, "Let him go, he's lost 'em!"

Streaked with sweat and winded from tearing round after the beasts, Herbert and Alfred were relieved to see the last one cut. Fritz still stood holding the bucket. He had had the best end of this job.

"Now what with becket?" he asked the farmer, using part words and part pantomime. "In muckheap?"

"Good God, no!" The farmer was truly aghast. "I'll have them fried for my breakfast tomorrow," and he mimed cooking, and eating. Fritz at length understood, and it was his turn to be truly aghast.

"Mein Gott! Ballocks!" he said, but the farmer did not read the revulsion writ large upon Fritz's face, and thinking to give him a treat, he fished in the bucket for a handful of pink testicles, and wrapping them swiftly in a clean handkerchief, he gave them to Fritz, and said, "Here! Get your camp cook to fry them for your breakfast! Lovely! You'll enjoy that!"

Poor Fritz was overcome with repugnance, but did not wish to give offence, so he worried all the way home, sitting in the lorry, with the soaking bundle of rag in his pocket.

"He can't mean it!" he kept saying. "He can't really mean he is going to eat... them! What a barbarian!"

"Well you don't have to if you don't want to," Herbert said, reasonably. "Chuck them overboard. I don't think I should fancy it myself...?"

The time had come to introduce the prisoners to a more flexible working arrangement. The powers-that-be had decided that it was possible to allow one or two of them to live out on the farms. This reduced transport costs, and this would obviously be acceptable to certain farmers who could get more work done by having chaps around all the time. Another alternative was to allow prisoners to go to work, in ones and twos, using bicycles.

The idea fired the imagination immediately, and Alfred was jubilant.

"Just think, mate!" he shouted, shadow boxing an unmoved Herbert. "Our own transport! We can ride around at leisure. We could wander up and down the lanes all day! Bloody marvellous, that'd be! Course, we shall have to turn up at work some time... but we could go the long way round!"

"I don't reckon they'll let you get off that easy," Herbert said. "There are bound to be some rules, regulations, or bloody orders, so just calm down."

"I haven't had a bicycle since I was a kid," said Alfred, allowing a wistful note to creep into his voice.

"You're still a bloody kid," grinned Herbert, "and another thing, don't forget that here you will have to ride on the wrong side of the road."

"I'd forgotten that… but I'll soon get the hang of it."

A couple of days later, two bicycles were issued from the labour office, and mid-day rations were in bags on the back of their saddles. Herbert and Alfred mounted and set off.

"Mein Gott! But this is great," Alfred shouted over his shoulder, as they pedalled madly along. The wind reddened his cheeks, and his blonde bush of hair stood up round his ears as if meeting some kind of challenge. Just for good measure, he stood up on his pedals, and raised one hand above his head. Then he got cocky and free-wheeled with his feet on the handlebars.

"Doesn't it feel great not to be watched over all the time?" Herbert called, attempting to steer some kind of straight path, and wobbling all over the road in the process. It was fortunate that the approach road to the camp was deserted at the time, for it had been years since either of them had been on a bicycle.

When the cycles had been issued, everyone receiving them had been briefed about not getting lost, and making sure that they returned at night. But, to prisoners who had been locked behind barbed wire, and only taken out under

155

guard for such a long time, it was almost freedom! The sensation of not being watched over was almost a physical thing, like the shifting of a weight. Alfred's spirits were greatly uplifted by this, and he capered about until, as was inevitable, he ended up on the grass verge with the bicycle on top of him. But he was not quelled, and he got up, dusted himself down, and remounted without even losing the broad grin from his face.

"For God's sake, ride the bloody thing properly, and let's get to work," said Herbert testily. He was feeling a trifle insecure on his machine, and when they reached the main road and saw traffic whizzing past them on the 'wrong' side, he felt more apprehensive.

Eventually, they launched themselves into the traffic and arrived safely at the farm where they were to work. They had been sent here before, and more or less remembered the way. They liked this farm, and got on well with the farmer and his wife, who, kind soul that she was, always tried to find them a little extra in the way of food.

She had a son away in the army, who had been fighting in Germany, and for whose safe return she prayed daily. His photograph stood in the place of honour on the kitchen dresser, and she had showed it to Herbert and Alfred, with some pride. He was a nice, clean-looking young man, with a mouthful of large white teeth, and his hair sleek and flattened with brilliantine.

"Ja! Good!" they had said, handing it back, and giving it a quick polish on her apron, she replaced it on the dresser. She bore no resentment towards these Germans, even though they were the ones her son had been fighting. They were all just 'boys' to her, and she hoped that somewhere, perhaps some German woman would show her lad some kindness, if necessary. A kind of simple, uncomplicated philosophy that took no account of politics. They liked her.

Occasionally they were asked to stay on to work a bit late, perhaps to finish a job, or help with a bit of clearing up. On such nights, the farmer would notify the camp that they would be late, and they would always be provided with a good meal before they set off on their cycle ride, often a packet of cigarettes as well. The meal provided for them back at camp would be gratefully consumed by their less fortunate comrades, and Herbert kept his fags for trading.

As he cycled along behind Alfred, it was getting dusk, and Herbert thought that this 'bicycle lark' was working out just great. The sense of freedom was an undoubted morale booster, and they were picking up quite a bit of the English language. Alfred stopped pedalling.

"I'm so full of grub, I can hardly push the bloody pedals round," he called back over his shoulder.

"Great!" grinned Herbert, slowing down. "Push off!"

The next day, back on the same farm, sometime around mid-afternoon, Herbert, wielding a muck fork and whistling 'Unter den Linden', suddenly realised that he had not set eyes on Alfred for the past hour or more. Where the hell was he? He gave a half-hearted shout, but no one answered. Where the devil could he have got to? He flung down the fork, and thought he had better see if he could find him. He was supposed to be here, helping him.

He looked in the nearby cow-bier, but that was empty. He looked in the loose boxes, and called Alfred by name, but the only sound to be heard was the scratching of a few hens in the yard. He looked in the barn and the tractor shed, but there was no sign. He stood stock still, as a thought unwittingly flashed across his brain. Surely the silly bugger hadn't run off? Not at this stage? Come to think of it though, he had been a bit quiet last night in the hut, and he hadn't heard from home for a long time. He had mentioned this fact only last weekend, and Herbert had said not to worry too much, the mail was unpredictable, and he would probably get several letters all at once.

Herbert knew that Alfred had a young and pretty wife back home in Germany, to whom he had been married only a few short weeks before he was captured, and he worried a great deal about her. Where was she? What was she doing? And was she still safe? He usually went very quiet for a bit on such occasions, and then, being Alfred, he talked himself out of this mood and capered about, being a 'card' more than ever.

Surely he wouldn't be so daft as to try and get back home on his own now? Still, you never knew with Alfred. He was a bit 'up in the air' at times, but by God there wouldn't half be some trouble if he had gone missing.

It would certainly put an end to their new-found comparative freedom! Herbert rushed round to where they had left their bikes that morning, and was relieved to find that they were both still there. Well, at least he hadn't pinched the bloody bike!

He'd better have another look to see if he could find him, and if not, he'd just have to tell the farmer, he supposed. He wandered around the farm, looking into all the outbuildings, and bawling 'Alfred' at the top of his lungs. He poked his head into sheds, behind doors, and even looked under hedges, and in the hay loft, but to no avail.

He was really worried by now, and he could have cheerfully strangled the silly little bugger! At length, he went into the empty bull pen. He could not imagine why on earth Alfred should have gone into it, but... a search is a search. The pen, at first glance, appeared empty, but there was a strange smell in there which, just for a moment, he was quite unable to identify. It seemed strangely familiar, and yet... he couldn't think where it came from. Then he remembered! Cider! A fruity alcoholic smell!

He strode over to the corner which was screened off by a stack of straw bales. Three large barrels of cider stood on a wooden trestle, and from beneath it appeared the booted feet of Alfred. A couple of empty bottles were rolling about in the straw, and a gentle, rhythmic, bubbling snore disturbed the silence. The picture was clear.

"You bloody fool!" Herbert groaned, and bending down, he caught hold of Alfred's ankles, and dragged him none too gently, from under the barrel.

Alfred's eyes remained closed, and Herbert gazed down upon his recumbent form.

"What the hell do I do now?" he muttered. He slapped at the round red face with the flat of his hand, turning it from side to side, in an endeavour to wake him. But Alfred was well and truly pissed, and did not flicker an eyelid. God! If anybody catches him like this. He's obviously pinched the bloody stuff anyway... He grabbed Alfred by his stocky shoulders, and shook him. His head lolled from side to side, and a faint grin hovered around his mouth. Herbert had an inspiration. 'Water!' he thought. 'That'll teach him!' He grabbed a galvanised pail, belted back into the yard and filled it with ice cold water from the outside pump. He ran back into the bull pen, and with some glee, dashed the entire bucket full right into the face of the dormant Alfred.

This brought forth some sign of life, so he repeated the process. Alfred came-to, spluttering and cursing.

"What the hell...? What did you bloody do that for...?" He shook the water off his head, like a wet dog, and the effort brought forth a groan. "I'm soaked.... Soaked!"

"You silly sod! You're pissed. Sozzled! High as a bloody kite..." Herbert shouted at him. "How much of the stuff did you drink?"

With a sweeping gesture, Alfred indicated the empty bottles.

"I think... quite a drop," he said. "It's damn good!" and he belched loudly.

"I hope you're sick, and I hope you have a bad head," muttered Herbert with feeling, and grabbing hold of Alfred beneath his arms, attempted to stand him on his feet. "Stand up! Get on your feet, you fool," he hissed. Alfred made a feeble effort, then sank down again, and clasped his head in his hands.

"Oh! My God! I can't," he groaned, with a depth of feeling.

Herbert looked at him in exasperation. It was obvious that Alfred was not going to get mobile that quick. He'd have to sleep it off somewhere. He was unceremoniously dragged back into the corner, behind the straw bales. Herbert dragged some of the straw over him so that he wouldn't be conspicuous, and went back to finish his own work, and Alfred's. By dint of chatter, silly questions, and any other ruse he could think of, he managed to divert the farmer from enquiring as to Albert's immediate whereabouts, or from suddenly deciding to go into the bull pen, until with relief he realised that it was time for them to set off back to camp.

When he went to fetch him, Alfred was recovered somewhat, although not entirely, and with Herbert gripping his offside arm, with fingers like a vice, he managed to walk a reasonably straight line through the yard, and around the side of the house to collect their bicycles.

"Cheerio, lads!" called the farmer, with a half-hearted wave, as he went towards the house.

"Cheerio!" they shouted back, and waved, Herbert manipulating Alfred's arm, like that of a glove puppet, since he didn't seem to be able to make it move by himself, and collecting the two machines, they headed towards the road.

Once out of sight of the house, Herbert heaved a sigh of relief. So far, so good! If he could only get this silly ass back to camp, the whole escapade might go undetected.

It took them a long time, since they had to walk most of the way, Alfred being incapable of steering a straight course on his feet, let alone on his bike. Twice he collapsed into the ditch, and was hauled to his feet by an unsympathetic Herbert. He would have left him there, but for the fact that they would probably both lose the new-

160

found freedom afforded by the bicycles. All Alfred could say was "Oh! My bloody head!" The fates were on their side, for they managed to get through the gate, and right back to their hut without any undue attention. Once inside, Herbert shoved Alfred on to his bunk, pulled off his boots, threw a blanket over him, and left him to it.

Gunter Westhauf had managed to land himself a really cushy job in Camp 31, working in the quartermaster's stores, outside the wire compound, dealing with both British and P.O.W. clothing. Sergeant Miller was ostensibly in charge, and after the initial period of suspicion, he and Westhauf got on well together. Westhauf was intelligent, and picked up quite a lot of English fairly quickly, so that in a comparatively short time, they could hold a reasonable conversation. Westhauf always managed to look well turned out, smartly dressed and groomed. He was, in fact, rather vain - the peacock syndrome – even if the only people he had to parade in front of were his fellow prisoners. But then, if he couldn't be well turned out, who could.

These stores were no different from many others in that a lot of fiddling went on, of all kinds. It was amazing what forty cigarettes could produce, and Miller was always on the lookout for free fags. Westhauf paid careful lip service to all his foibles, being assiduous in carrying out his orders to the letter, whilst at the same time, he ran a very profitable little racket on his own account. At the end of the month, when it was time for the routine check, Westhauf cooked the books a little, slightly amended the stock lists, slipped Miller a few more fags, and everybody was happy!

A mere few miles from the camp was a Women's Land Army Hostel, and every Wednesday night, a dance was held in the village, attended by most of the girls in the hostel. Miller never missed this function, and kidded himself that he was making good progress with the girls. He thought himself no end of a chap, and spent hours getting himself ready to go out, sleeking his hair with

Brilliantine, trimming his little black eyebrow moustache, and pressing his trousers. On the Thursday morning, he would recount details of his conquests, his sexual hand-groping, and fumbles in the back of the car, to the sceptical, and in truth, slightly envious Westhauf.

One morning, after Westhauf had listened with feigned admiration and attention to a further twenty minutes of 'The Miller's Tale', the sergeant impulsively turned to him and said, "You're not a bad sort, really! You'd look quite good in some decent clothes, and you don't speak bad English now! Tell you what! Strictly against every rule in the book of course, but if you keep your trap shut, no one need ever know! Next Wednesday, I'll lend you a British uniform, and you can come with me! Eh! Meet some of the girls? Have a bit of fun!"

Westhauf was truly astounded, and thought at first that he must be joking. The British sense of humour again!

"Of course," Miller continued, 'I can only lend you a Private's uniform. Anything higher wouldn't be right!" And his voice had a slight moral edge. He apparently took Westhauf's astonished silence for acceptance.

'He must be bloody drunk,' thought Westhauf, 'or else hungover! I'll never get away with that!' But Miller was not to be put off. If he wanted to do someone a good turn – which was not very often – then he'd damn well do it!

"Be all right," he said, seeing the disbelief on Westhauf's face. "Course it'll be alright! Leave it to me!"

Westhauf was torn. On one side was his desire to keep in with Miller, just in case Miller decided to take offence and put a stop to his profitable little rackets. Besides, he rather thought it would be a lark, and he could have some fun. He was a young man, and it had been a very long time since he had been out with a girl. Female company was conspicuous by its absence at the camp, obviously. He also thought it a wry twist that he, a German prisoner of war, should be tripping the light fantastic in a British private's uniform, when only a little while ago, he had been shooting at that very uniform. On the other hand, if he was

162

caught, and put in the 'cooler' for twenty-one days which seemed to be fairly minimal, this would effectively curtail his trading profits, and even cause him to be transferred to another, and far less desirable job.

Miller took his acceptance (and his gratitude) as a foregone conclusion, and at half past seven on the following Wednesday, Miller, with Westhauf dressed in his borrowed uniform, set off in Miller's ancient Austin 7 to go to the dance. Westhauf felt strange in the unaccustomed clothing, and had to fight back his desire to hide behind Miller. As they parked the car, the sound of a four piece band issued forth from the open doors of the village hall, with the customary 'knife-and-fork' beat of the amateur drummer. Inside, the festivities were in full swing, and the hall was already packed. The weight of numbers comforted Westhauf, who thought he could perhaps escape undue notice among all this lot.

"We'll go and have a few dances first," Miller told him. "Pick up a couple of birds!" His close-set eyes roved around the room. "There seems to be quite a bit of talent here! Then, after that we'll make for the nearest pub. They only have tea and soft drinks here, and who the hell wants that on a night out?"

Miller strode off with a purposeful gleam in his eye, but Westhauf hung back a little. He was feeling very unsure of himself, until the band began what they fondly imagined was a 'slow' waltz, and he found that he knew the melody. Summoning all his courage, he selected a likely looking girl, and asked her to dance. As they circled, the floor seemed a little bumpy to him, and he was undoubtedly out of practice, but he persevered, sweating slightly. He mentally rehearsed several phrases in English, but felt relieved that the noise from the band, and the whirling couples, effectively prevented much conversation.

The floor was uncomfortably crowded, so that they could not help but occasionally bump into other couples. The girl didn't seem to mind, she just held on tighter and smiled, swaying in time to the music, closing her eyes, and with what Westhauf considered to be a particularly vacuous expression on her face. He hoped she wasn't getting any ideas about this.

At the next bump, he turned round with the usual word of apology, for he was nothing if not polite, and found himself looking straight into the face of the camp interpreter, Staff Schneider! He missed his step, and thought 'Christ! This is it,' waiting for the hand of authority to descend upon his shoulder. But "Sorry, mate!" said Schneider, and carried on expertly twirling his partner around the floor.

'He must have recognised me,' Westhauf thought, as he once again caught hold of his partner, and resumed the dance. 'Perhaps he just doesn't want to create a ruckus here, in front of everybody, and spoil the whole evening. Well! What the hell? If I'm caught, I'm caught... let's enjoy ourselves.'

Half an hour later, Westhauf and Miller sat having a quiet drink in the local pub with a couple of the girls, when Westhauf excused himself to go to the lavatory. As he emerged from the door marked 'Gents', Westhauf froze, and felt his face flame. "Relax," Schneider said. "I'm not on duty... and who cares anyway?"

Westhauf made his way back to Miller and the girls. He thought perhaps that he ought to mention to Miller that Schneider was here, and had both seen and recognised him, but he found it difficult at this moment to say anything. It would sound so daft in front of the girls, to whom he was a British soldier called Tom, who talked with just a trace of a faint accent, and whose phrases were over-polite and rather stilted. Schneider had told him to relax so he, Westhauf, would obey that order.

As he lay in his bunk that night, he thought about 'his' girl. June, she said her name was! What kind of name was that? She was a bit 'full-blown' with big breasts and rather thick thighs. And she was a bit hot-arsed! He and Miller had driven the girls back to their hostel, and there had been a bit of parking in a convenient field gateway. The vigorous necking that had gone on had almost been his undoing after such a long time! June had a rather wet, loose mouth, and had drenched herself in some heavy, sickly smelling perfume, which had not covered up entirely the faint odour of B.O. She had wound herself around him with a grip like a boa-constrictor, but he hadn't minded too much at the time! He reflected complacently, that he must still have something, hadn't quite lost his old touch!

It had been a smashing evening, he really had enjoyed himself, and it had done wonders for his ego! Good old Miller! Westhauf hoped he would suggest the same thing again. Perhaps it would be as well to wangle him a hundred free fags, in the morning?

Camp 31 was manned at the main gate by German POW police, who did a four hourly shift, right round the clock, six days a week. They were billeted outside the camp, opposite to the lorry park, where they had a Nissen hut, all to themselves. Their duty mainly consisted of patrolling the main gate, checking upon all and everything entering or leaving, and twice a week, two of them accompanied the ration truck to the Supply Depot to collect the food for the entire camp.

There were six of them, but as things transpired, one of them had to leave. Rumour had it that he was being sent home on compassionate grounds, but this left a vacancy and it was a job that was considered quite 'cushy'.

"Why don't you apply?" Heinemann, the band leader, suggested to Herbert. "It'd be a damn good thing. Dead easy! Just think! Four hours on duty, and the rest of the day is virtually your own. You could put all your extra time in with the group then, and as you know, they could all do with it."

Herbert thought. "What about night duty?"

Heinemann waved this aside. "That's easily fixed! You can always trade a few fags, and buy a swap, can't you?"

"Do you think I should get it?"

"I don't see why not! Somebody's going to get it, why not you?"

"Well..." Herbert was undecided. He didn't like these quick decisions, but Heinemann made up his mind for him.

"Come on," he said. "We'll go and see the chief now. We'll tell him straight up how important it is that you should have more time to spend with the theatre group, and he's sure to pull strings. Come on, what are you messing about at?"

So, Herbert was given the job. He was briefed about his duties, and responsibilities, and told that in future he was Camp Police No. Six. Once again, he collected all his bits and. pieces into his kit-bag, and moved into the Nissen hut, the German Camp Police headquarters. He found it very roomy for only the six of them, and comfortable too.

The chief explained about the rota, and about rations and the cookhouse, and told him not to worry about a thing. He'd soon settle in, and get the hang of it. He was much older than Herbert, and patted his shoulder paternally.

"We're just like a big family in here," he beamed. "Very comfortable. Oh, we have our duties to perform, and we do them, and we do them efficiently, make no mistake about that. But, we do them in our own way. No one disturbs us, and no one asks questions. That's the way we like to keep it. Oh, you'll soon settle down, and enjoy this job. Smoke?"

"No thanks, I don't." Herbert felt quite at ease, relaxed, and stretched his legs out in front of him. This time, it appeared that he had got hold of a cushy number.

A blue armband with a white letter 'P' on it, to be worn on the left lower arm, was issued to him. The duties were, in truth, very simple, and he soon became familiar with the whole set up. He began to feel the benefit of his eight hours of free time, and planned to have a go at writing – a thing which he had often given much thought to, especially at night as he lay in his bunk, but which he had never before seemed to be able to find the time for, nor the

166

necessary quiet and privacy. He was sure he could manage a simple play for the theatre group to perform. It would have to be a comedy, of course! Something not too complicated, and relatively easy to stage. He had worked out with the other camp police that his free nights should coincide with meetings of the group, and they had all been very co-operative about swapping duties, and working occasional doubles. Herbert thought it was damn good of them.

One morning, as he stood on duty by the main gate watching the day's working parties slowly leaving the camp in an assortment of vehicles, the Tommies descended and made a surprise check. One party of ten prisoners were pulled out of the convoy and bundled into the guardroom where a thorough search was made.

Somehow, the British had got wind of the fact that the prisoners were making children's toys inside the camp, then smuggling them out via working parties, to be sold to people on farms and around for English money.

This was definitely not permitted. It went dead against the grain. The British seemed to turn a blind eye to much that went on inside the camp, and they must have known more than they let on about the trading in fags, pinching from the stores, food smuggling and so on, but by some strange quirk of nature, this business of the toy making had really got them worked up.

With uncanny accuracy the guards picked on the right working party, and when the search was completed, it revealed two little wooden trucks, a box of building bricks, and a fabric mouse. All were beautifully made, finished, and with the wooden toys painted in bright colours. Things to delight the eye of any child. The working party had not actually had any hand in their manufacture, but were merely acting as agents and doing the selling, doubtless for some commission! The toys were immediately confiscated, and the 'agents' sentenced to fourteen days in the 'cooler'.

Herbert privately thought that this made the price of delivery a bit high, and was rather surprised at the severity with which the British regarded the incident. Not that it made any real difference, for the manufacture continued, but the delivery was held up for a week or two.

When Herbert came off duty, and returned to his billet, he found that the post had been, and an envelope, addressed in his mother's handwriting, lay waiting for him on his bunk. At the sight of it, the almost despairing feeling of homesickness returned, and he felt a vague apprehension, almost real fear, and he hesitated to open it. He wanted news of his family, but if the news was not good, and he was here locked up and powerless to help, it would almost be worse than knowing nothing.

He turned the letter over and over in his hands, but then with an exclamation of impatience, he tore it open. It had been censored, as usual, but there were only two lines blacked out. It was quite a long letter really, especially coming from his mother, who was invariably terse and to the point in her correspondence, and to whom letter-writing was a chore rather than a pleasure.

His brother, Fritz, was living at home now, with his parents, she wrote, and his wife and their baby. They had been bombed out in Dresden, but thankfully, they had not been injured. Fritz had walked all the way from Dresden to Hamburg to see if the family home was still intact, and if he could bring his family to live with them under one roof. Then he had walked all the way back again to fetch them, and their few belongings that they had managed to salvage from the wreckage of their home. There was no transport of any kind to be obtained for love nor money.

The house in Hamburg had been burned by an enemy incendiary, she said, but it was still habitable in part, although they could not use the upstairs now. Even if they could, there was no fuel to warm the house, and no repairs could be carried out because there was no material to do any repairs, so the hole in the roof and the shattered windows had to stay. Anyway, they were all living together now, and they were managing very well, considering everything.

Father was home, but had lost much weight, and he was not well enough to work at anything. She was trying to get him to rest as much as possible. But, they were alright, and he was not to worry about them, because he was a prisoner anyway, and he could do nothing to help... They all sent much love, and they were all longing for the day when he would be sent back home. 'We think of you every day,' his mother had written, 'and we thank God that you are still alive, and that all of us, the whole family, have come through this terrible war, so far...'

There were many gaps in their circle of friends, and many neighbours that he would not see again. There was much bomb damage, and he would not recognise some of the streets... She hoped to get a letter from him soon, which would give her renewed strength to carry on until the day of his return...

Herbert read the letter through again and again, and conflicting emotions formed a hard lump in his chest. He had a mental picture of the house in Hamburg, as he had last seen it; the plush curtains with fringes on them that were hung at the windows in winter time. He had got into real trouble once when he was a kid for cutting off some of those fringes to decorate his music stand! He thought it looked great, just like the stands that were used by real musicians in big orchestras, and he had been careful to cut them off on the inner edges, hoping that they would not be noticed... at least until spring came, and the plush curtains were replaced by lighter flowery ones. It had been the usual punishment. Confined to the house for three weeks! Not that he was, of course. He and his brother had an arrangement, and the lavatory window was always left open so that he could climb in and out, and cover up for each other.

Then there was that pretty girl a couple of doors up the road. What was her name? Hilde! Yes, Hilde! He had been forbidden by his father to have anything to do with her, he was not even supposed to talk to her, and he never found out why. When he asked, his father merely replied that she was not 'suitable' and had refused to be drawn any further.

Not that Herbert had taken much notice. He had, as usual, done exactly what he wanted to do, but he had been careful not to get found out!

This letter brought memories flooding back in minute detail, and he felt unbearably saddened. Nothing could ever be the same again. This he knew and accepted. He was not the same himself, not at all the same young man who had joined the German army. The life of 'before the war' was gone forever, and Herbert didn't know if he was prepared to settle for less. He didn't know how he would be able to cope with going back to Germany, cope with missing friends, the changed scene. He felt that he would be a stranger in his own homeland, for they would all have had experiences in which he had no part, just as he had been to places, done things, seen things in which they had no place. Their lives had gone on, but upon divergent lines, and the past now seemed so unreal. Home itself seemed unreal. The Nissen hut, the prison camp, fellow prisoners had now taken the place of family, and become his real world. The other one he no longer knew, and although he longed to go home, as they all did, he could not help but feel apprehensive.

Nobody, he reflected with unaccustomed bitterness, would come through this lot unscathed, whichever side they had been on, and for whatever reason they had fought. It was just not possible to emerge untouched. True, he supposed, scars must eventually heal over and thicker skin must form, but beneath this new skin, the flesh would be forever tender to touch.

"Mein Gott," he told himself. "Why are you lying here getting bloody morbid? You are not free anyway, and you

170

stay here until 'they' decide whether you go home or not! So bloody get on with it!"

He replaced the letter in its envelope and stored it away safely. Then, striding purposefully out of the billet, he walked energetically around the camp, eventually making his way to the place where he could always lose himself - the theatre!

Hut No.3. was generally referred to throughout the camp as Monte Carlo, for it was a veritable gambling den. Cards were played in friendly games all over the camp, and in every hut, but the occupants of No.3. were fanatics. They gambled on anything, and everything. How far they could spit, or pee, flies crawling up the wall, anything that moved, or anything that they could make to move. Any visitor to the hut, whether just making a friendly social call, or on official business, got roped in if he wasn't careful. Almost before you could open your mouth to say 'hello' either you were in some game or other, staking your all, or you were asked to leave.

The stakes were high, and almost anything would be taken in payment. Gamblers frequently ended up minus their trousers, their underwear, their boots, fags or a month's pay. Food of any description was staked and well received, and even girlfriends for a 'one-night-stand' on the prisoners return to Germany. Cards, dice, darts, draughts, and chess went on all the time, and then they obtained a roulette wheel. From then on Las Vegas looked like a Sunday school bun fight compared to Hut No.3. Long after 'lights out' little groups continued to play by the light of candles until the early hours of the morning, until they fell into their bunks, bog-eyed, bleary and minus pretty well everything.

One particular Sunday morning, the casino was in full swing. Bets were being laid, and cards dealt. IOU's on scraps of paper changed hands at an alarming rate, and there was no other topic of conversation. No one even mentioned women, sex or the state of the nation, and had they done so, they would have undoubtedly have been told to 'Piss off!'

Klaus Klinger was one of the hut's permanent residents, and he liked a game of cards just as much as anybody else, but he was damn fed up with all the intensive gambling that had developed. It was getting tedious. It was getting so that people didn't talk anymore. Nobody said anything to anybody else, unless it was to place a bet on something or other. All the 'friendly' part had gone out of the game, and gambling fever had taken over completely. Now, winning was all important. Nobody was a good loser, only a temporary loser, and they all meant to get their own back when chance offered.

The atmosphere in the hut, even when they were all supposed to be relaxing, was thick with tension. Klinger was fed up with it all. He tried mentioning that it was all getting a bit out of hand and whatever had happened to conversation but they all told him to shut up and push off, scarcely troubling to look up from the whirling numbers, or the falling cards. He did not like it, and in fact, he was beginning to feel exceedingly uncomfortable and ill at ease in his own hut. He wondered if there was anything at all he could do to make them see how daft they were all behaving! How seriously they were taking themselves. He would have to try something, or, if that didn't work, he would have to try and get transferred to another hut. Damned if he was going on and on like this! This gambling fever was as real as a physical disease.

Then he had an idea! Klinger's mind was a tortuous one, and the whole thing was rather silly really, but... it was a protest. A demonstration! And he thought it worth a try. He got off his bunk, and fetched a fire bucket from outside the hut, placing it carefully in the gangway. It was half full of water.

What he needed now was a long piece of wood. A broom handle, that might do! In the corner stood the very thing he was looking for, and with a swift knock off came the broom head, leaving Klaus holding the stale. Now for a piece of string. Homemade washing lines might have a bit that would suit? Five minutes later, he had his bit of string. He picked up his little homemade stool, put on his overcoat, and put a little tin box carefully in his pocket. Then he went towards the fire bucket. The string was tied to the end of the broom handle, a bent pin was tied on to the end of the string, and on to the pin was fixed a crumb of dry biscuit from the tin box. He took off his overcoat, and folded it neatly, for he was a methodical man, and he sat down on the stool. Slowly, quietly, and with consummate care, he lowered the string, pin and bait into the bucket, and sat there looking at it fixedly.

So far, none of the other occupants had taken much notice of his preparations, mainly because they were all dicing fast and furious, so Klaus was left in peace. More than an hour passed, and still he remained, gazing at his string dangling in the water. The broom stale was still clutched in his hand, but by now, the dry biscuit bait had disintegrated into 'sog'. One of the other inmates of Hut No.3. rose from his gambling game, having lost all he had to stake, and stretching, strolled over to him. No movement from Klaus. The other chap watched him, puzzled. Then he touched him on the shoulder.

"You feeling alright?" he asked.

"Shhh," Klaus put a finger across his lips. "Don't make so much bloody noise!"

The chap drew back slightly, and looked hard at Klaus. "What the hell...?" Then, backing all the way so as to keep Klaus in sight, he went over to his mate, and whispered, jerking his head in the direction of their fellow resident. The other man arose, and they both strolled towards Klaus. They peered at him, searching his face, but he did not even blink. What the hell was up with old Klaus? This wasn't like him! Good, steady sort, old Klaus!

"Nothing wrong, is there?" the second chap asked.

"Shhh," Klaus said.

One by one, the gamblers at the other end of the hut got to their feet and came to see what was going on. Klaus remained unmoving.

"You feeling upset about something?"

"You a bit homesick?"

"What the hell are you playing at?"

Klaus looked up in some irritation. In silence he stood up, unfolded his overcoat and put it on, picked up his tin and broom handle, and turning to the others he said, "Among all your blasted gambling, surely a chap has a right to enjoy a few hours quiet fishing? When I was at home, I always went fishing on Sundays. But... if you won't be quiet, I might as well go home anyway. It's a pity they weren't biting very well..." and he strode back towards his bunk at the end of the hut. Then, turning, he said, "You might not realise it, but you have not gambled for at least ten minutes! You have spoken without laying a bet. What a bloody change!"

The others looked at each other, and then a roar of laughter, with some relief in it, ran through the hut.

"You're bloody barmy, Klaus," they said, and one tapped the side of his head significantly. And then... "What a good idea! A sort of fishing contest! In a bucket! We could make a book on the best catch of the hour... That'd be a new one...!"

Poor old Klaus sighed in the corner! Ah well, he had stopped them for ten minutes, but there was obviously no cure. He looked round his 'home'. He would have to see if he could get a transfer, he really couldn't stand all this tension. Pity! But still, there it was!

Hut No.3. had one particular ritual which was rather unique, and which could only be invoked for gambling debts and nothing else. The more they played, the higher the stakes, and there was almost invariably someone who could not pay up. A rapid and whispered consultation would then take place, and the hapless chap would be told that his account would be settled, and the slate wiped clean, if he agreed to take the Holy Ghost! Not entirely

174

understanding what this was, and no one would tell him, he almost always agreed.

It was necessary for this event to take place in full view of the entire hut, or it did not count. A table was placed in the centre of the gangway, and spread with a blanket. One of the inmates took up his position at the head of the table, and held aloft a lighted candle. The victim, or that is to say, the debtor, was brought forward with ceremony, his trousers removed, and he was laid down across the table, eyes towards the floor, and his bare backside exposed to the gaze of all.

One by one, the entire hut filed slowly past, and gave him a resounding slap until by the time everyone had had a turn... and those to whom he owed the most were allowed more than one go. His buttocks were red, sore and stinging. The operation was then finished off by applying black boot polish to the exposed area, liberally in great daubs, and it was rubbed well in. He was then said to have been 'polished off' and the man with the candle declared his account to be 'clear'.

When this pitch was reached, the poor sod made a concerted dash for the washroom in an attempt to scrub himself clean, and was often to be found there more than an hour later, sitting with his backside in a wash-basin full of cold water. It was not an easy matter to get the blacking off anyway, and it usually took several days before the last trace of the 'Holy Ghost' disappeared. But then, said Hut No.3., if you can't pay up, don't gamble.

Rehearsals for the Christmas show were in full swing, and the theatre group were working really hard. They were to present a comedy in three acts, written by members of the group, and entitled 'My Mother-in-Law', and as may be imagined, it contained every possible double entendre and innuendo that they could get into it. Behind the scenes, carpenters and painters were already struggling to make all the scenery Herbert required, and to transform the bare stage into the opulent set of a Victorian mansion drawing room. A lot of new costumes were needed, and this meant that the tailor too was being kept busy.

Herbert was really pleased at the progress made by 'his' group, and he was grateful to them for their enthusiasm and for the hard work they had put into the whole thing. They had pulled together well, and operated as a team, not seeming to mind his bawled instructions, and his 'What the bloody hell do you think you're supposed to be?' or 'You move about more like a Shire horse than a woman! Don't clump your feet!' He thought they deserved a little celebration of some kind, a sort of 'night out with the boys' after the performance. He felt they had earned it, and in any case, it was traditional to have a party after the first night, wasn't it?

Being Herbert, and with lingering memories of his earlier disastrous efforts to save one dry biscuit a day until Sunday, his thoughts naturally turned towards food. Some kind of feast! A table lavishly spread. He had a word with the cook, who was both sympathetic and helpful, but "meat's the problem," he said.

"I can usually wangle a few extra stores here and there, but not meat. There is never enough meat," said the cook.

"What would you like?" Herbert asked.

"Well," said the cook wistfully, and with the air of one remembering good things long past. "Some lamb, or perhaps a bit of mutton would be nice!"

'Difficult,' thought Herbert, 'but not totally impossible!'

Willi Zander was the singer with the band. He was a tall, thin chap with rather nice light brown wavy hair which he combed and pushed into place frequently, even when he was talking to you. As a singer, he was not really up to much, but he could belt out a few of the well-known sugary songs, and this always went down well with the audience on concert nights. He never seemed to suffer from any nerves either, so that when there was a hold up back stage, it was easy to say 'Send Willi on to sing another number' and Willi did, more or less holding the fort until the next part of the entertainment could begin. He combed his hair between each song, and stood fairly still, singing with his eyes half-closed, crooning from his throat as he fondly imagined Bing Crosby did. This gave the whole thing rather a comic effect, but the audience always responded, and he was very popular.

He was very good-natured too, so that when he heard on the camp grapevine about Herbert's needs, he came up with the answer. "Look mate," he said, "I'm working on a bloody sheep farm all day long, aren't I? Surrounded by the damn things! And I've seldom seen a dafter animal. Of course I can organise a sheep for you! No trouble! You leave it to Uncle Willi!"

"Don't be stupid," said Herbert tersely. "You can't pinch a whole bloody sheep! How are you going to get it back into the camp for a start?"

"All will be arranged," said Willi, grandly.

"Now look, forget it," Herbert said. "We shall all get it in the neck if they catch you, and if you yourself end up in the cooler on the night of the concert, then I will personally have your guts for garters. Myself."

"For Christ's sake, shut up," said Willi. "Leave it to me. I can't truthfully say that I have ever done much sheep rustling, but it can't be that hard. When do you want it?"

"Get out," said Herbert, and Willi went.

When Willi Zander went to work the following morning, he had fully made up his mind that he was going to get a sheep somehow. He carried beneath his arm a rolled up sack, but this occasioned no comment, for working parties frequently carried sacks so that they could bring back with them pieces of wood from the various farms and fields to supplement the fuel ration for the huts. Only one bucket of coke per day was officially allowed, and wood made a valuable addition to this. In Willi's pocket was a half sharpened table knife 'nicked' from the canteen.

All day long as he went about his work, he turned over and over in his mind ways and means of catching the animal, and once having caught the damn thing, how to finish it off.

By mid-afternoon he was no further forward, but he thought he had better make some kind of start, since the lorry was due at four thirty to take them back to camp, and this didn't really give him much time. He ambled over to the field where the sheep were peacefully grazing, and he sat down beneath the low stone wall bordering the pasture. He combed his hair thoughtfully. They were fairly slow-moving creatures, he thought. It might not be so difficult.

He selected one ewe which seemed to his rather inexperienced eyes to be fairly young, and thus, hopefully, tender eating, and rising to his feet, began to stalk her. He moved slowly so as not to startle the animal, but every time he got within three feet of her, she darted away, twitching her ears.

He tried from the front, the animal skittered sideways. He approached from the rear, and she darted forward. Like partners in some lunatic mazurka, he and the sheep covered the entire field, until the rest of the flock, sensing the panic of one of their number, decided that they would all join in, and bunching up together, skirted the field at a fair trot, bleating. Willi followed at a graceful gallop, his booted feet slipping in the mud. The unaccustomed exercise was making him sweat, and meanwhile, he was keeping a weather eye open in case the farmer should be around and wondered what was upsetting his stock.

Willi decided that this could not be the right way to rustle a sheep. He knew that the farmer had a dog for doing all this work, and in fact had watched him on more than one occasion, guiding the dog by a series of whistles. It had looked dead simple to Willi, so he had tried to make the dog move, whistling in exactly the same way as the farmer seemed to, but to no avail. The astute animal had totally ignored Willi's whistles, and the farmer had grinned.

"It's no good you trying," he said. "Wrong language!" And pointing at the dog said, "He's Welsh!" He had laughed uproariously at this, and Willi gave up.

Willi gave up chasing the flock round the field, and sat on top of the field gate to think the thing out scientifically. He combed his hair again which, in his case, was always conducive to clarity of thought, and toyed with the idea of bits of string and wire to make some kind of snare. He cast aside the idea of a net as being impracticable, and was just working round to a length of string with flat stones tied on to the ends of it, and used as a bolas, when he realised that the sheep were once again stationary. One was grazing very close to him, and he watched it intently.

As he sat on the top bar of the field gate, immediately below him was the usual winter quagmire always to be found in farm gateways, and this stupid animal was standing right in it, nibbling the grass from around the edges. If anything was necessary to confirm the perversity of sheep, this must be it, Willi thought. He sat quite still, his comb and his right arm suspended a few inches above his hair. The only sound was the gentle squelch of the mud as the sheep moved slightly to reach the juicier tussocks of grass.

Willi silently loosened his feet from the bars of the gate, tensed himself, and momentarily balancing like a trapeze artist, he launched himself into space, straight at the unsuspecting animal. The sheep, oblivious, knew nothing until she was flattened by the flying Willi, and they were both spread-eagled in the mud of the gateway. Willi's comb flew out of his hand, and he got the sheep in a kind of half-Nelson. The prey struggled violently and set up what Willi considered to be an inordinate amount of noise. They rolled about together in the mud, and he clutched her muzzle in his free hand in an effort to keep her quiet.

Now what should he do? He had to turn this live animal into a dead carcass somehow. He freed one hand, and reaching into his pocket, found his knife. He closed his

179

eyes, and plunged it into the sheep's throat, hoping that he would hit the right spot. He had no idea of where the right spot should be except in the general area, but he knew there was a vein that had to be cut. A jet of warm blood covered his arm, and the sleeve of his tunic, and he was rather astonished because he had never given much thought to this aspect. But the animal was dead!

With some difficulty he rose to his feet, striving to gain a foothold in the mud. He hadn't realised that a damn sheep would be that heavy. He looked down at the carcase, but forbore the urge to plant his foot upon it, and give a Tarzan yell. Instead, he retrieved his sack from where he had hidden it under the hedge, and attempted to get the meat into it. The sheep was slippery with mud and blood, and so was Willi, but the thing was accomplished, and he packed handfuls of loose grass into the sack hoping that it would prevent the blood soaking through and attracting attention.

He attempted to clean some of the mud off himself with handfuls of grass, but he didn't make a very good job of it, and he hadn't much time left. He could hear the unmistakeable sound of the lorry thrashing and revving up the lane. Shouldering his laden sack, and whistling, he made his way to the pick-up point.

Back at the camp, Herbert was on duty at the main gate. The returning working parties were perfunctorily checked over by the Tommies, and let into the compound. Willi looked a sorry sketch.

"What the hell happened to you, Zander?" the Tommy said.

"Fell in mud," Willi answered, and executed an admirable pantomime to emphasise his point. "Not serious. Not hurt! I wash!" and grinning, he strode on, the sack on his shoulder.

Herbert, witnessing this little episode, felt the back of his neck go hot and red. It was obvious to him that it was not wood in the bulging sack that Willi carried with what he fondly imagined to be an air of nonchalance! It was the promised feast! 'The silly bugger's done it!' he thought. As Willi passed along in the file of returning workers, he tapped the side of his nose, and gave Herbert a leery wink. Herbert had heard the English use the expression to 'bring home the bacon' and decided that this must be the German version.

When he went to the theatre that evening, after his duty, he found that the carcass had been hidden beneath the stage, and Willi and another chap were at this moment busy skinning it. It was, by now, 'clack' cold and stiff, so that they were having quite a job with it, both being totally without any previous experience in the art and skill of butchery. By the time they had finished, and cleaned out the entrails which they dumped in fire buckets, it was well after lights out, and the last of it was accomplished by the aid of candles.

The sympathetic and co-operative cook was waiting to receive the meat, and stashed it away for safety, but he baulked at the offal. In fact, he flatly refused to accept the innards or the skin. The carcass only was what he was going to deal with and nothing further. Muttering slightly at the lateness of the hour, he disappeared from view, wearing dead mutton slung around his shoulders like a silver fox!

"Not to worry!" said Willi, ever cheerful. "We'll shove it back under the stage, and work out what to do with it tomorrow."

And once more he loped stealthily back across the compound with two fire buckets full of steaming and malodorous guts, followed by the others with the skin, head, feet etc.

The following night, after they returned from the day's work, the conspirators lit the iron stove in the rehearsal room behind the stage of the theatre, and when a roaring fire had been made by means of nicked wood, they began to dispose of the guts. These were dropped into the flames, a little at a time, and the resultant smell was beyond belief.

The fleece was cut up with the aid of a pair of nail scissors, and as it burned, the fat from it ran down the inside of the stove in fiery rivulets. Black smoke belched forth from the tin chimneys above the hut, and inside their eyes watered from the acrid fumes. They coughed and spluttered, until in the end, they had to agree to take it in turns to stand outside and draw in lungfuls of air. The camp was screened by black smoke for most of the night, but fortunately, the prevailing wind was away from the British quarters, or there must certainly have been some investigation. Fortunately too, perhaps, it was one of the Tommies' birthdays, and he had brought a few bottles into the camp, so that they were not paying too much attention to anything outside.

The last of the fleece and guts was burned in the early hours of the morning, and everybody fervently hoped that the last traces of black smoke would be dispersed before the morning roll-call.

The cook, good as his word, provided them with a real feast, and the night out with the boys was an unqualified success. But, God, how the smell lingered! For two weeks afterwards, whichever entrance you came into the theatre your nostrils were assailed by the stink of burning mutton fat. Herbert quite liked it, and Willi became insufferably full of himself over the whole thing. For a while, anyway.

As Herbert entered the theatre one evening, his ears were assailed by the sound of hammering on metal. Hans Bauer, one of the group, was on his knees on the floor engrossed in the design and manufacture of some contraption, which Herbert at least, failed to recognise.

"What the hell's going on?" he asked. "And what's that thing supposed to be?"

"That's my friend," said Hans, looking up. "Is going to be a 'distill. I've been finding out all about it, and I'm going to have a go at brewing whiskey!" He was obviously plainly excited at the idea.

"Mein Gott! Just you wait. When I've got this thing working, we shall be alright! You won't be able to tell the difference between this, and the real stuff! Honest! This is the way they make whiskey anyway... only on a much larger scale of course."

Everybody else looked dubiously at the debris lying around on the floor, and at Hans disbelievingly, but he refused to allow his enthusiasm to be quenched. "You just wait," he said with conviction.

He had already collected some canisters, a few odd lengths of assorted piping which just happened to have been left lying around here and there, and which he was sure no one would miss, and a few empty bottles, already washed out, for his first brew. He had done some welding with a poker, heated to red hot in the black iron stove, and had knocked off some wheat, barley and a few potatoes.

He had always been partial to the occasional tot of whiskey, and now he could scarcely remember when he had last had one. But he could remember what it tasted like. He could almost feel the caramel coloured fluid on his tongue, sliding gently over his tonsils, down the back of his throat, and the glow of warmth in his belly. He dwelt upon this fantasy, and at the thought that this past delight may soon once more be within his grasp, his eyes glazed over, and he gazed blankly into space like one moonstruck. Then he set to work again, and his enthusiasm was infectious. Suddenly, everybody was willing to help old Hans start brewing.

When the distillation was completed to Hans' entire satisfaction, and he was very careful about this, they all met again in the rehearsal room, with the windows suitably blacked out. The stove was red hot, and on top of it sat the still. It was the focus of all eyes, and when at length it started to boil, a subdued cheer went up from the assembled multitude.

Hans, with eager anticipation writ large all over his face, quietly got to his feet, and tip-toeing over the intervening floor area, carefully placed one of his clean bottles at the end of the pipe, anxious that not one drop of the precious liquid should be wasted. Then, smiling all around, he tip-toed back, and resumed his seat.

Everybody sat there, waiting. "Come on my little beauty!" said Hans, almost crooning. "Show us what you can do!" Nothing seemed to be happening.

"Throw some wood on the stove," said a voice from the rear. The canister gurgled, hissed and bubbled with almost a maniacal fervour. The stove seemed to shake with the heat, and above it the air was a-shimmer with the glow from the burning wood. At length, and very slowly, a drop of topaz coloured liquid slid down the tube and dropped into the waiting bottle, to be followed by more at rhythmic intervals.

"Look! Look!" Hans shouted, waving his arms in the air and executing a minor war dance all around the steaming contraption. They all looked.

"It really looks like whiskey," said someone in tones of awe.

They gathered around, and approached as close as the heat would allow. They could almost taste the brew, it looked so good. Then, suddenly, the drips stopped.

"It's gone off the bloody boil! Shove some more wood on!"

The still continued to bubble and hiss, and the heat was almost molten, but... no more drips.

They looked at each other in consternation, seeing the promised tot of whiskey rapidly vanishing. Seconds passed, and then, the air in the hut was split asunder by the sound of an almighty explosion. Everybody instinctively threw themselves flat on the floor, their arms covering their heads, while the last traces of echo bounced back from wall to wall.

It seemed as if there was only going to be the one explosion, and gingerly they looked up. The still was no more! The entire room was covered with a mixture of wheat, barley and potatoes, walls, ceiling and floor. The black iron stove was littered with fragments of metal and debris. They looked at each other. Everyone had a liberal coating of the whiskey 'mush'. The heat from the stove had not abated, and to this was added the smell of burning where the filthy stuff landing on the hot surface was rapidly charred to a cinder.

Hans got to his feet, and wiped the worst of the mush from the front of his hair. By some quirk of fate, the bottle containing the first few inches of his precious whiskey was still standing, and it was still intact. He picked it up, and took a gentle swig.

"Not bad!" he said. "Not bad at all!" and he handed the bottle around.

A close examination of the remains revealed that the narrow outlet pipe had been blocked by some coarse grains of wheat, but Hans' confidence was not the least bit shaken, and he was sure he could repair it and start again.

"I shall make some slight modifications to my original design," he announced to his muttering and cussing compatriots, all busy scraping the muck off themselves. "We – using the Royal plural – "shall try again."

"Not while I'm about, and not in my bloody rehearsal room," Herbert decided, as they started to scrape the walls.

CHAPTER IX

The Beginning of Repatriation

The word was going around on the camp grapevine, nothing official, that repatriation was shortly to begin, and the whole compound buzzed with the news. Plans were made, taken up, talked over and discarded with amazing rapidity. Everybody was looking forward, obviously, to being reunited with their families and what they were going to do when they got there was nobody's business. Schemes ranged from fantasy to total bizarre. Every meal time, the conversation took the same turn: 'We are going home at last.'

When they eventually learned the truth, it caused intense disappointment. The ones destined for early repatriation were those over the age of fifty-five, those in poor health and not able to do a day's work. However, volunteers were badly needed for work in the German coal mines, and if prisoners would sign an official agreement to work for at least twelve months down the pits, arrangements would be made to send them home in a fairly short time.

The response to this was, in fact, quite good, and a lot of the prisoners whose only thought was to get back home at almost any price, volunteered for this work. Herbert and Alfred talked it over, but the idea did not impress either of them. Alfred desperately wanted to get back home and he thought constantly of his young wife, but "I can't stand it," he told Herbert.

"I know I couldn't. I can't stand being in confined spaces, and in the dark. I get claustrophobia, and then I get scared, I'm actually sick. It's no good me thinking about it, I know I just couldn't do it."

"Well, I'm not that bad", Herbert said. "But even so, I don't think I could do it either. A year down a bloody pit would just about finish me off, I think." He pushed his thoughts far away. Then turning to Alfred, whose usually cheerful face was rather pale and worried, he said, "We've stuck it this far, we might as well stick it out to the end. It can't be that long before they send us all home. I'll wait."

Two weeks later, the first batch of prisoners left the camp, and started on their way through endless transit camps, and red tape, on their way home. Herbert watched them go, and wondered if they realised what they were going back to. The occupation forces would be very much in command. Germany had suffered a terrible defeat, and they would find very little in the way of work they had once been used to, the life they had once led. But still, they were going home, and perhaps to them, this was all that really mattered.

Herbert and Alfred were sorting through the accumulation of props and costumes in the rehearsal room. They had acquired quite a bit of stuff here and there, some of which could be made over for use again, and some of which was no damn good to anybody.

"We shall have to have some more costumes for the next show," Herbert said. "We need some black stuff."

"That's easy," said Alfred, a grin splitting his face from ear to ear. "You know that big house just outside the camp? The bloody place is empty! Has been for some time I think. And they've got no end of blackouts fixed up at all the windows."

"You can't break in there and pinch that!"

"I don't see why not! The place is empty. Nobody is living there, and they are not going to need the blackouts again, are they?" Alfred said, reasonably.

"That's all very well, but... Breaking in!" Herbert was very dubious about this.

"Oh, leave it to me," said Alfred. "The damn place is empty, has been for a long time, and nobody is going to want to use the stuff are they? So we might as well, mightn't we? How much do you need?"

"I don't want to know anything about it," Herbert said.

"All right!" Alfred was exasperated. "Don't bloody well know anything about it. But... just don't be surprised if it turns up!"

A few nights later, in the early hours of the morning to be exact, Herbert was on duty, patrolling the compound on the outside perimeter, when he heard a faint rustle in the bushes. He stood stock still and listened. All the nights, and all the times he had been on duty, and never once had anything happened. He heard it again. Actually, he was not too sure what he was supposed to do if he ever discovered anybody trying to break in or out of the camp! As he watched, a shadowy shape appeared from the same direction as the sound, and it was struggling with what appeared to be an unwieldy bundle.

"Halt!" said Herbert, feeling that at least he ought to do something, after all, he was on guard duty.

"Oh, shut up you fool," hissed Alfred. "Don't just stand there! Come and give us a hand!" He was slightly breathless with his exertions.

Herbert was apprehensive. "What the hell have you been up to now?"

"For God's sake, shut up! Unless you want the whole camp to hear. Just give us a hand."

"How did you get out?" Herbert hissed. Under the cover of darkness, Alfred's look was pitying.

"Through a hole in the wire a bit further up," he said. "Didn't you know it was there? I think I must have made it a bit bigger now though. And I've torn my bloody sleeve!" He gingerly felt the rent up near his left shoulder. "Now, if you've finished your daft jabbering, perhaps you'll give us a hand to chuck this bundle over the wire into the compound. Then I'll go back the way I came and retrieve it. Then you can fall back into your trance..."

Between the two of them, they managed to get the bundle over the wire, and heard it fall with a soft thud inside the compound.

"Right! See you later, cock," and Alfred made off quietly, back the way he had come. Herbert carried on with his patrol.

'Bloody hell!'' he thought. 'I told him to forget it!'

When he came off duty, he made straight for Alfred's hut, and together they made their way to the theatre where Alfred had stowed the bundle, once again beneath the stage.

"There's plenty of good material there," he grinned. "A lot of blackout stuff, and... I brought some blue velvet curtains as well!"

"Oh my God!" groaned Herbert. "There won't half be some trouble if ever they find out."

"Balls! You're too whiney, that's your trouble! Just be grateful that I went out and got it for you!"

Looking through the bundle, Herbert thought they would have enough stuff for costumes for at least the next three shows.

There seemed to be yards of it, and it was pretty good. It had faded in streaks where the sun had caught it at the windows, but even so, it was better than they had got hold of before. The best thing to do, he thought, was to get it cut up so that at least it was more easily able to be hidden, and hopefully, would not be so recognisable. He'd better get it over to the tailor's shop, as soon as he opened up. That was the theory, but things didn't quite work out like that.

About three o'clock that afternoon, a police car drew up outside the commandant's office. Herbert was again on duty, and seeing this, he put two and two together, making the usual four and a half. Alfred must have been spotted! He hadn't been so damn clever after all! He looked around in vain for some means of getting a message to the tailor's shop to get the stuff out of sight, but all the working parties were out, and there wasn't a soul about. He even

189

contemplated leaving his post, but reflected that if this was discovered as well, it would merely add to all the trouble he felt sure was at this moment brewing

An officer and two policemen came out of the commandant's office, and headed towards the main gate. They looked straight at Herbert, and he felt himself grow tense, and the hairs on the back of his neck stood up. But they took little notice of him, and disappeared into the office of the Lagerführer. They must have stayed in there a damn long time, as well, because they had not emerged when Herbert had to come off duty.

When the working parties arrived back at the camp, Herbert was sitting on Alfred's bunk waiting for him.

"You've done it this time he said, anger sharpening his tone. The police have been here today, and I'm damn sure it must be because somebody has reported a break-in at that house. I told you it was a daft idea! Now you come with me, and let's get rid of the stuff before anybody can find it!"

"What the hell are you going on about?" Alfred, having just returned from work, and tired, was disposed to be testy. "What are you getting your knickers in a twist for? Even if they do find it, how are they going to know who took it? Anyway, you don't even know if that's what they are here for! It could be something entirely different! For Pete's sake, shut up about it! And get your own bloody stuff next time!" Herbert gave up and left him to it.

Next morning as the camp assembled for the usual roll-call, by the side of the Lagerführer, the bundle lay on the ground. There was no mistaking it, and there could be no mistake. That particular tell-tale bundle, black tied with bag string, and bits of dark blue velvet readily visible. The chief addressed them:

"Yesterday afternoon, I had a visit from the police! I do not intend to make a long-winded speech about it. By the side of me, you can all see this bundle of cloth. It was found inside the camp! It is therefore painfully obvious that one or two of you must be responsible for its presence

190

here. It is stolen property, and was taken from the big house not far from this camp.

"I hope I can trust those guilty of this to come forward and take their punishment. The commandant has ordered me to bring the person or persons responsible to his office by nine o'clock. I hope I can do that, and that it will not be necessary for the whole camp to be punished. That's all I have to say to you, and now it is up to you."

Alfred had listened to this speech, wooden faced. Out of the side of his mouth, he muttered to Herbert, "That's bloody well torn it! Well! Lamb to the slaughter, and all that muck! You stay where you are!" Before Herbert could even mutter a reply, Alfred stepped forward. "I'm responsible," he said. The Lagerführer glared at him.

"Report to my office," he commanded.

Alfred vaguely wished he had listened to Herbert, and left the whole damn thing alone. Ten minutes later, flanked by two officers and followed by the Lagerführer, Herbert saw him being marched towards the commandant's office.

The sentence was a bit sharp. Twenty-eight days in the clink, on bread and water, and... what was worse, the camp theatre was closed until further notice.

At first, Herbert was so furious with Alfred for making such a mess of things that he felt not the slightest twinge of sympathy, but as the days progressed, and he thought about the bread and water, his anger evaporated somewhat. Poor old Alfred! No bloody grub! And he was dead keen on his food, poor little bugger! And he was only allowed outside for thirty minutes a day for exercise. That was all he would see of the outside world for twenty-eight days.

Herbert hung around a bit, unobtrusively he hoped, and caught a glimpse of Alfred after about ten days inside. He was rather pale and noticeably thinner. There wasn't much that Herbert could do about it. The sentence had been passed, and Alfred would just have to sweat it out. The only thing was, could he get some food into him? The bread and water diet would be a great hardship to anybody like Alfred, and if a few extra bits could be smuggled in

191

somehow, it would help. It wouldn't be easy, though. The clink was rather heavily guarded at all times. The cell block was outside the wire, and there was not much cover either.

Herbert obtained a large slice of fruitcake from the canteen, and cut it into small pieces. He carefully wrapped each cube of cake separately, and then wrapped all the little parcels inside his handkerchief. He decided that if he went around to the cell block, through the hole in the wire, when he came off duty at eleven o'clock, he could reach up and push the parcelled cubes, one by one, through the mesh that covered the bars of the cell block window. There should not be much activity anywhere in the camp at that time of night, and if he was lucky, he might just get away with it! Again... he was wrong.

He managed to make it just beneath the cell block window without being spotted, by the simple expedient of crawling flat on his belly, and rising cautiously to his feet, he stood still, listening. An owl hooted nearby, and a light breeze stirred the branches of the trees.

"Psst! Alfred! It's me!" he said in a voice that he hoped Alfred would hear, and nobody else. "Alfred! Are you there? I've brought you some grub!" He unwrapped his handkerchief bundle, and reaching up as far as he could, he tried to push through the first cake cube. At that precise moment, a beam of light from a hand-held torch shone full on his face!

Like a flash, he dropped his parcel, and flung himself face downwards on the ground, the cubes of cake scattering in all directions. His heart was beating like a sledge hammer, and he dare not make a move. 'Oh! What a bloody mess, what a bloody mess' kept on running through his brain.

The light continued to shine on him, and he felt a hand roughly grab hold of the back of his collar. It was all up, he thought, and so rose voluntarily to his feet.

"What the hell do you think you are up to?" It was the voice of the commandant. Herbert found himself totally unable to answer that one.

"In my office in the morning!" the voice rapped out, and the light was extinguished.

"God," thought Herbert. "It would have to be him. What the hell is he doing prowling around at this time of night?" He learned later that the commandant had, in fact, a habit of doing just this.

The following morning, flanked by two MPs and followed by the poor old Lagerführer, the party headed towards the commandant's office. Herbert stood to attention. The commandant didn't bother to ask any questions, but contented himself with glaring balefully at Herbert.

'Come on! Get it over with!' Herbert said, silently.

"Put this man back on to farm work immediately! Cap on, left turn. Quick march!" and Herbert was once again outside. He was rather relieved, and considered that it could have been much very much worse. He could have ended up in the cell next to old Alfred, and quite honestly, this was what he had expected. Well, if it had to be farm work, then so be it!

As they headed back, he looked towards the cell block. 'Sorry mate!' he said mentally, to the incarcerated Alfred. 'You never did get your bloody cake, did you?'

On the 8th February 1947, Herbert clambered on to the back of a truck, his bits and pieces once again all gathered together in his kit-bag. It was snowing! Great whirling flakes which melted instantly when they touched his red hands, and the collar of his coat. The snow had changed the landscape, softened all the sharply etched outlines of the trees and hedges, muffled all the day-to-day sounds, blurred the horizon. Everything looked cleaner and new-washed somehow, and gentle.

The truck began to move, and crouched in the back under the torn canvas cover, he watched Camp 31 slowly disappear from view.

CHAPTER X

Back on the Farm

The truck laboured along with some difficulty. The snowfall was increasing, and the wheels were forcing it into deep, packed ruts. Drifts, like carelessly flung pieces of cotton wool lay against the hedges. Herbert, sitting despondently alone, looked out over the tailboard at the whirling flakes, and remembered a paperweight that someone had once given to his mother for a Christmas present a very long time ago. It had a little miniature garden inside it, with tiny flowers, rose trees, and a summer house, but when you shook it, the entire garden was covered in snow. He remembered how he had loved that little thing, but his mother would only allow him to shake it once. He supposed that if it had been broken, all the water would have gone all over everywhere.

The truck turned, skidding in the ruts, its wheels spinning uselessly just for a second, until the driver recovered it, and then drove off down a farm drive.

"I thought you would never get here," came the voice of Klaus Klemp, who emerged from the saddle room, already enveloped in his overcoat, and carrying his kit-bag.

"You're damn lucky we got here at all," Herbert retorted. "Twice we nearly skidded into the ditch, and once we got stuck in the snow. The bloody roads are likely to be blocked solid before dark!" He slapped Klaus on the back. "What's it like around here?" he asked. But Klaus refused to be drawn.

"You'll find out soon enough," he said.

For some reason, things had not worked out well on this farm for Klernp. Nothing concrete, it seemed, but some slight clash of temperament, some incompatibility, and he had asked to be transferred back to the camp. Therefore, following Herbert's misdemeanour, it seemed the logical thing to swap them over. Klemp refused to elaborate on any of this, and merely said that he was damn glad to be going back to the camp, and his face wore a non-committal expression.

'Oh! Sod it anyway!' Herbert told himself. If he had not been sent here to take over from Klemp, he would have been on bread and water in the cell block, so what the hell!

The truck driver signalled that he was ready for the return journey, and Klaus clambered on board. As the truck moved off towards the farm drive, Herbert suddenly remembered something he had meant to ask Klemp, and he ran after it, waving both arms, and slipping frantically on the snow. "Klaus! Eh, Klaus! Which side of a cow do you have to sit to milk it?" Klemp waved the question aside. "Please yourself," he said, and settled back as the truck gathered momentum.

Herbert was now alone, at least for the time being it seemed, and he took the opportunity of having a look around him. He could undoubtedly be categorised as a 'survivor' and it was only this facility that had kept him both sane and reasonable so far. He was not of the type that spent hours in futile speculation, and in wishing things to be different. He often did wish things to be different, but fleetingly. He usually looked at any situation, summed it up, and if at all possible, turned it to advantage. If he couldn't, then he stuck it out until it changed of itself.

He was doing this now as he looked around the saddle room which had been in the occupation of Klaus Klemp, and which was now to be his. It contained a small stove, which was rather dirty, and stone cold. Apparently, it had been alight, but had been allowed to go out. There was a camp bed in one corner. Apart from what seemed to him to be an inordinate amount of 'tack' the room contained no other concession to personal comfort.

He could not help but feel slightly depressed. The whole world suddenly seemed so damn cold, inside and

196

out. He leaned on his arms and rested his forehead against the dirty window pane. It was still snowing. He was a bit concerned now about his lack of English. At the camp it hadn't seemed to matter very much because there was always the interpreter, and it was always possible to talk to fellow prisoners. But he was the only one here. If he couldn't speak much English, and nobody else here could speak German, and there was no reason to suppose that they could, he would have absolutely no one to talk to! Privacy was one thing, but isolation was different altogether. The few English phrases that he had picked up were not quite suitable for polite conversation anyway!

The door opened, and an arm encased in a tweed sleeve appeared, and in the large hand on the end of it was a steaming half pint mug of tea. "You the new chap then?" the disembodied voice said. "Milking time now, okay? Finish your tea first!" The arm withdrew and the door closed. Herbert was grateful for the tea, and cupped the tin mug in his icy hands. He began to feel a bit better, and the hot liquid was making a comfortable pit of warmth in his belly.

'Cowman, I suppose,' he thought. 'I shall have to face him sooner or later... better be now.'

The sound of cows who knew when they should be milked, and knew their way to the byre, led him to the right place. Twelve Red Polls and one Jersey were tied into the stalls.

"I suppose you can milk?" came the disembodied voice from somewhere at the other end.

"Yes!" lied Herbert, and decided not to let on that he had never even been up close to a cow before, let alone milked one!

"Take that one at the end," the voice went on, and waved a vague hand. Herbert picked up a bucket and stool with the air, so he fervently hoped, of one who knew perfectly well what he was doing, and approached the animal. Carefully seating himself, he placed the bucket beneath the heavy udder, and grasped the teats. 'Now

197

what?' he thought, and the bovine head turned towards him, and moist brown eyes gazed at him reproachfully. Nothing else happened. He squeezed vigorously. Nothing! The cow made a noise in her throat.

"Sorry old girl," muttered Herbert.

"Finished?" came the voice of the cowman.

"Not quite," said Herbert desperately, looking down at the totally empty bucket. The cow raised her muzzle, and gave a low moo.

'What the hell's the matter with her?' thought Herbert. Perhaps she hadn't got any inside and he peered intently at the swinging udder. He had been given the briefest of instructions before leaving the camp. All of which had gone in one ear and out of the other. Now confronted with the real thing, he wished he had listened.

The cowman came from the other end of the byre to see how he was getting on. He was a short square man, with a face like a crumpled brown paper bag. He looked at Herbert and began to laugh, looking for all the world as if the brown paper bag gaped wide open, and the sound that issued forth was like that of the Royal Scot getting up steam.

"You're doing it all wrong," he wheezed.

"I don't think I'm doing it at all," Herbert said, in German.

"What you do is pull and then squeeze," the cowman went on, and he demonstrated with two hands held out in front of him. "What you're doing is squeeze and then pull! No wonder the poor beast won't let her milk down!" He chuckled and wheezed his way back to the other end of the byre.

Next morning, Herbert met the boss. Immediately he understood why Klaus Klemp had not got on very well here, for the boss was, at least to German eyes, the epitome of Englishness. He was, for what the term is now worth, a 'gentleman'. He was of abstemious habits, high principles, and pursued a policy of total honesty towards all. He went in for quality rather than quantity in everything, but fortunately for him, he seemed to be able to afford to do so. He wore a good suit, owned four cars, six hunters, and... thirteen cows! He employed a cowman, gardener, cook-housekeeper, daily cleaners to do rough work and a groom.

This lot would have been, to Klaus Klemp, like a red rag to a bull, for he was the complete antithesis of it all, and moreover, mentally at least, he was still fighting the war, and the British in general. Herbert and the Boss weighed each other up as they met, and Herbert knew that if he kept his nose clean, he would be treated all right here.

Herbert's meals were provided by the cowman's wife, and used to the rather rough, overcooked camp fare, he was delighted to find the food provided, although simple, well cooked and plentiful, much of it from the kitchen gardens. He set to work to make his own quarters warmer and more comfortable, but here he ran up against the groom, who still persisted in regarding it as more or less his own exclusive territory. He had an annoying habit of just walking in, with thick mud all over his boots, and dumping the 'tack' down anywhere. This was an anathema to Herbert's tidy German mind.

In vain he tried to keep the place in order, constantly cleaning the floor, and hanging up the offending 'tack' on the pegs provided, but he found himself becoming increasingly irritated at the man's apparent uncaring attitude.

Herbert liked order with a capital 'O'. He liked everything to be carried out with neatness and precision. He preferred garden paths to be straight, flowers to grow in orderly rows, and to the same height. If he hung any pictures, he measured the exact depth from the ceiling, from the floor and from each corner. Everything had to be just so, to be right or he didn't feel comfortable about it. Even his camp bed was made exactly so that each blanket had the same amount of tuck-in, and the corners neatly squared off. The groom was obviously of an entirely different temperament.

What Herbert really wanted was some kind of room all to himself. Entirely his own. After years of sharing Nissen huts with others, of constant communal living, the thought of privacy seemed like an unattainable Eden. He pondered at great length upon possible ways and means of achieving this.

There was an empty loose box in the stable yard that had not been used for livestock for some time, and it was now full of all kinds of odds and ends that had been just dumped in there for convenience. He looked it over, and thought that if he could obtain permission to do so, he could convert this into very comfortable quarters for himself, without too much difficulty. This would give the groom full and unobstructed use of the saddle room to make as much mess of as he wanted, and this would probably please him as well!

Herbert talked to the cowman, not without difficulty, but he had by now acquired a tattered and dog eared copy of a school's German/English dictionary, and by means of looking up almost every word, and not bothering too much about grammar, he conveyed his request for the use of the loose box.

The cowman talked to the Boss, but they were not all that keen on this idea. They said that loose boxes were for animals, and were totally unsuitable for living accommodation, even – as they put it – for German prisoners. However, after a little pressure, they gave in, shrugged, and said that Herbert could do as he liked.

'Right!' he thought. 'Just give me a month, and they won't recognise the place.'

Every night, after he had finished his chores around the farm, he was hard at it in his new home. He scrubbed the accumulated muck of years from the floor, walls and roof, and used gallons of boiling water, and a great deal of elbow grease.

He painted the dirty greyish discoloured walls with the remains of a can of yellow paint he found in the stores, and he whitened the ceiling. Some heavy grain sacks were washed out, sewn together and laid on the floor as a carpet. He 'found' some suitable pieces of wood and made himself quite a reasonable looking level table, whilst a couple of deck chairs 'borrowed' from the summer house in the garden provided comfortable seating that could be folded away when not in use. The cowman donated a paraffin stove, and his wife some net curtains to cover the window. A lamp shade was contrived from a piece of heavy paper carefully folded into pleats, and the otherwise bare walls were liberally decorated with pictures out of magazines, the subjects wide and varied – whatever took Herbert's fancy at the moment.

He moved his camp bed into his new quarters, added his meagre personal possessions, and took up residence. It felt great, and for the first time in years, Herbert thought that if he closed the door, he could really get a little privacy. The cowman and the others around the place seemed to appreciate this need, and never walked in without knocking, or without invitation.

Herbert showed his 'cottage' to the Boss, with some pride, just to let him see what ingenuity can do, and the Boss was obviously impressed, as Herbert had intended that he should be. He complimented Herbert, and told him to let him know if there was anything else he needed.

According to the rules governing the use of Prisoners of War for farm work, the pay was still five shillings a week, as it had always been, but not in money. It was paid in goods such as razor blades, soap, cigarettes etc. From the first week of Herbert's arrival at the farm, the pay had been eighty cigarettes a week, and anything else he wanted had been given to him as and when he asked for it. Quite soon, as he was a good worker, he was given a hundred and fifty fags a week, but the funny part of the whole thing was that he didn't smoke!

And there was very little trading he could do here. Every week he stored away his 'wages' until the cupboard in the corner of his quarters was bulging with the store of cigarettes. He occasionally gave some away, but he still had far too many. It hardly seemed worthwhile starting the smoking habit just for the express purpose of using up his store of fags.

What he really wanted was a watch. His own had been taken from him when he was captured, and he really missed not knowing the time, especially now that he was working on his own. He worked out the cost of the cigarettes he was given each week, and thought that if the Boss would give him the money instead, it would only take him about three months to save up enough to get himself a timepiece. The trouble was that the Boss was not supposed to give him money, only goods, but the more Herbert thought about it, the more reasonable it seemed to him.

He decided to mention it to the Boss, and every time he saw him, he attempted to begin his carefully rehearsed little speech, but he lacked the confidence. Another month slipped by, with Herbert poring over his tattered dictionary, until he eventually managed to take the plunge, and tell the Boss of his plan. The Boss listened, and then said "I'll see what I can do" but Herbert was not at all sure that he had made himself clear.

He worked extremely hard that week, but when pay day came he was again given his hundred and fifty cigarettes, and he thought that obviously the Boss had not understood, or perhaps did not agree. 'Well it was worth a try! Let it go!' he told himself, once again packing his wages into the cupboard.

Three months later, to the exact date on a Tuesday morning, the Boss came into the yard, and handed to Herbert a small parcel.

"Here you are! Don't drop it," he said, grinning.

Herbert put down his bucket and muckfork, and took the parcel in some surprise. He remembered to say 'Danke' and began unwrapping the brown paper. It was a brand new wristwatch, and the Boss laughed at the expression on Herbert's face.

"Well you did say three months, didn't you? I would gladly have given you one there and then, but... three months you said, and three months it is! You've worked damn hard, and I've had more than that amount of labour out of you, so... here you are!" He gave Herbert, who was having some difficulty in expressing himself, a friendly pat on the back, and went off, still chuckling, and in fact rather pleased with himself.

Herbert was grateful, not only for the watch which would be of great help to him, but also for the way in which the Boss had given it to him, and the way in which he had handled the situation, making Herbert feel that he had earned the watch, and not just had it given to him. And still the cigarettes kept on coming.

The cowman mentioned to Herbert, while they were both in the byre at milking time that three more German prisoners had come into the village to work on farms. He thought perhaps they might be mates of his, although he had no idea of the names!

After work was finished for the evening, Herbert was just leaving his precious loose box to have a quiet stroll around, which he did most evenings when the weather was good, when he saw three figures walking down the farm drive in his direction. They broke into a trot when they spotted him, and waved their arms, shouting in German. One of them had a bush of blonde hair sticking up all around his beaming face!

"I'll bet you never thought to see me out here," Alfred said, thumping Herbert soundly on the back. "When you left, I was still in that bloody cell block. But here I am. I'm not that easy to get rid of, am I?"

They spent the evening in Herbert's quarters, joking, catching up on camp news, and it was a great relief, especially to Herbert, to talk freely in his own language. Alfred was working on a local farm, 'without milking' as he said, Horst was working in the local mill, and Werner was fully employed with a large dairy herd supplying most of the milk for the surrounding locality, the farmer having his own milk round, Alfred and Horst were both heavy smokers, and Herbert was able to unload onto them some of his cumbersome store of fags.

The evening did not end until fairly late, and they all agreed to keep in touch, to visit whenever they could, and... to practise their English. Herbert felt relaxed and contented as he settled down in his camp bed that night. 'Fancy old Alfred turning up again, like a bad penny,' he thought. 'But that's just like him, he always does turn up...'

One evening, after they had eaten, the vet arrived in the yard. The boss, the groom and the herdsman were standing talking together outside one of the loose boxes, and Herbert gathered that a colt was to be 'cut' (that is to say, castrated). The animal was backed on to the stable door, a twitch put on his nose, and Herbert instructed to hang on to his tail. Before the colt could know what dreadful thing was to befall him, the vet had neatly performed the operation, and the two pink testicles were thrown into the yard. Herbert, mindful of his previous experience in this capacity, let go of the tail, and neatly fielded them into a bucket of cold water. He wondered vaguely if anyone had any ideas about having these for breakfast, but nothing was said on this score.

"That seems to be okay" the vet said, examining his handiwork. "Turn him out, and keep an eye on him for a couple of days. He should be fine!"

The next day was the groom's day off, and Herbert was asked to go into the field, and check if the colt was alright. Herbert didn't really know what 'alright' was. The animal was grazing, but as he moved forward, his hind legs seemed to be dragging just slightly. Herbert walked over to him, talking softly, and wondering if the thing understood German, to have a closer look. The colt swished his tail angrily at the flies buzzing around, but raised no strong objection when Herbert bent down to have a look at where the scrotum had been cut.

"Mein Gott!" he whistled, and set off back to the yard, running almost full tilt into the boss. He was a bit out of breath, and what with this, and his limited English, he had some difficulty in making himself understood.

"You come, boss," he panted. "Horse no good! Has grown!"

"What are you on about, Herbert?"

"Balls, Boss! Balls!" Herbert grew slightly incoherent.

"What?"

"Balls grow again. Come back! Greatly big!"

"Now don't talk silly," said the Boss impatiently. "You saw what the vet did yesterday, didn't you? And you know full well that testicles cannot come back!"

"No, sir! Horse not good! Big! Big as bloody little footballs!" Herbert's gestures to emphasise his point were a credit to his theatrical experience, and verged almost upon the obscene.

They both headed back for the field, and the Boss had a look for himself.

"You're bloody right," he said. "Good God, what's happened?" He was obviously as perplexed as Herbert. "Look," he said, "you bring the colt back into the yard, but gently mind, walk him slow, and I'll go off and 'phone the vet. He'd better come and have a look at this!"

The vet arrived in due course, and went into the loose box to check on his previous day's work. He emerged a few seconds later smiling broadly.

"Well?" the Boss said.

"No! They haven't grown again! The animal is not a scientific miracle! A wasp has stung him quite badly, right where I cut him. Poor beast! He'll be all right in a day or so, but keep him inside until the swelling has gone down!"

"Damn good job you noticed that, Herbert." The Boss was obviously relieved, for the animal was a valuable one, and Herbert, looking down at his new wristwatch saw that it was time for milking.

Herbert still did not get paid in money, but he had managed to acquire some, mostly in odd tips, and occasionally, very occasionally, the Boss tipped him a pound, like the time over the colt business. Down in the village, where he was now allowed to wander, he had noticed an old-fashioned type of draper's shop, which seemed to do a good line in odds and ends of second-hand furniture as well. Looking in the window one day, he saw a second-hand wireless set for sale. Immediately he realised just how much he wanted it. 'What a difference it would make to his cottage,' he thought. He could listen to all kinds of music, and he had missed music a great deal, and if he listened to talks and to plays, he felt he could be getting on faster with his English. If only he could manage to acquire this wireless set, there was no limit to its effect upon his life, and from then on, he thought of little else, but how to get hold of the damn thing.

He lacked the confidence to go into the shop himself, and ask what price they wanted, so he cajoled the groom into doing it for him. At least, that's what he thought he had done, but at half past five that evening, a battered green van drove into the yard, and braked with something of a flourish in front of the loose box. The driver alighted. "Baum-Hacker?" he said to Herbert, who nodded. "I have brought your wireless, sir!"

Herbert was dumbfounded. Utterly. Not only to be told that 'his' wireless had been delivered, but to be called 'Sir!'

"No! No!" he stammered. "A mistake! Not me!"

"It's a very good wireless, and a bargain at the price," the driver, who also owned the shop, was at some pains to point out. "I'm only asking £12."

"I no got so much money," said Herbert flatly.

"Well, if it suits you, you can pay it off a bit each week! I don't mind, if it accommodates you."

Herbert didn't know what to do, and he didn't know what 'accommodate' meant. He wanted the wireless very badly, but he also had an inordinate and disproportionate fear of debt. Never in all his life had he had anything without paying for it first, and the thought of actually owing money, and to a stranger, made him feel uncomfortable.

On the other hand, he could just see himself, basking in the warmth of the paraffin stove, relaxing in his deck chair, feet propped on the table, enjoying his well-earned and new-found solitude, while music issued forth from the wireless set, and carried him off into realms of nostalgia and fantasy. It was rather an ugly looking instrument actually, fashioned in a sort of sickly brown and yellow 'Bakelite', but to Herbert, at that precise moment, it was beautiful.

The little draper was beginning to get impatient with Herbert.

"Well, I can tell you", he said, "that you won't find no better bargain than this, and that's a fact! But still, if you don't want it..." and he picked it up to replace it in the van. Suddenly, Herbert saw this delightful object disappearing, and made up his mind.

"I have it," he almost shouted.

The draper was a non-smoker too, so there was no chance of Herbert paying off any of his debt with his accumulated hoard of wages. However, he gave the man as much as he could afford then and there, and made arrangements to pay off the rest at five shillings a week. It took him what seemed a very long time, and until it was finished, he never really felt that the thing belonged to him. On two occasions he had to miss a weekly payment, but the draper was very magnanimous, and he soon caught up when anybody, usually the boss, gave him another tip.

As the weeks slipped by, Herbert seemed to have acquired quite a few additional items for his 'cottage'. He had pegged a hearthrug from snippets of cloth, and using a sack as a base. He had contrived an imitation fireplace from a sheet of asbestos, with a wooden mantelpiece, and he now had a real armchair, rather worn and much used, but donated by the Boss. Herbert had repaired and tidied it up, and was well satisfied with the result.

Every Saturday afternoon he turned the place out, polishing, washing, scrubbing, cleaning everything in it. Then he laboriously did his weekly wash, and as a final touch, he gathered a few flowers from the garden, stuck them in a jam jar, and stood it on the window sill. He found that he was getting far too house-proud. 'Bad as a middle-aged housefrau,' he told himself, for when it was all cleaned up and everything in its prescribed place, he could hardly bear to go back inside in case he messed it all up again, and he would shamefacedly remove his boots outside, and enter in his socks.

There was just one thing about this that did not please him. The Boss was obviously impressed with what Herbert had achieved from such unpromising beginnings, and whenever he had guests staying at the house, which was fairly often, he would always bring them down into the yard to have a look at Herbert's room, and, of course, at Herbert himself. "Our prisoner of war!" he would say. He would point out Herbert's ingenuity with obvious pleasure, and Herbert would have to be on his best behaviour, make sure he had on his tunic, and be polite. He would smile, and bow a little from the waist, which they all seemed to expect him to do. After all, that's what all Germans did in films! Who was Herbert to be different? This preconceived idea of a German soldier rather amused him, and he said 'Ja! and 'Danke!' fairly frequently, but when they spoke to each other about him, as if he were not even there, confident that he would not understand, he almost laughed aloud.

One Sunday afternoon, the Boss arrived in the yard, with a party of three, and Herbert sighed resignedly.

"Here we go again," he muttered, and taking his tunic from where it hung behind the door, he put it on and tidied himself up in readiness. The boss showed them Herbert's cottage, and they seemed very interested, asking innumerable questions, which he did his best to answer with his few carefully learned phrases.

The next day, the boss pointed out the new gardener and his family. The daughter would be taking up the post of cook-housekeeper in the house, and the gardener and his wife would live in one of the cottages. Herbert found himself strangely pleased by this bit of news. He had found the daughter very pleasant and attractive, and he thought that it would be nice to have her around the place, for he could stand to see quite a lot of her. She had not spoken much, leaving most of the chatter and the questions to her mother, but as she left, she had turned back and smiled at him in a very conspiratorial way, as if she knew that he would have preferred to be left in peace, but was too polite to do anything but be agreeable.

She was exactly the type that Herbert had always admired anyway. Slim and shapely, but not too thin, with masses of very dark hair, well washed and smooth, that she wore shoulder length and tucked under in the current fashion. She had blue eyes that crinkled at the corners when she smiled, so that her whole face became momentarily animated. She looked impeccably clean, right through to the skin, and her grey coat and skirt were fresh and pressed.

Herbert had immediately become aware of the sad deficiency of his wardrobe, for he still wore the uniform of a prisoner of war, and although he always made sure that it was clean, and he pressed his trousers frequently, borrowing the iron from the cowman's wife, nevertheless, it had seen better days, and in places looked a bit threadbare.

If she was going to be around here from now on, there was no reason why he shouldn't get to know her, was there? They were bound to come across each other, for Herbert had occasion to go up to the house on numerous occasions. He wouldn't be at all surprised if these occasions didn't rapidly become more numerous. He had always been considered quite a personable young man, although some years as a prisoner had taken much away of his former self-confidence. If only he had a better command of English, although he was not getting on too badly. The cowman, his friend and mentor, said he was 'coming on a fair treat!' Although Herbert did not realise it, such English as he already knew, he spoke with a pronounced South-Warwickshire accent.

He laboured hard at learning English, for he suddenly found that he could not bear the thought that the girl might laugh at him and his stilted phrases. Worse still, she might refuse to speak much to him at all. There was no getting away from the fact that he was still a German prisoner of war, and that only very recently he had been engaged in fighting the English. She might even be married, have a husband who was in the army, or engaged or something. But somehow, he didn't think so. Suddenly, life on the farm seemed great!

"The Boss wants you up at the house," the cowman shouted to Herbert. "Now what's up?" Herbert muttered uneasily, for if the Boss had sent for him rather than coming down into the yard to have a word, it was obviously something of importance. He made haste up to the house, and into the Boss's study.

"Herbert," said the Boss. "You're going to be sent home! Home to Germany."

This news hit Herbert like a punch in the gut! For so long he had waited for someone to say just this to him, and now it seemed such an anti-climax. He could not reply. He waited to feel pleasure, delight, anticipation… but he felt nothing. The little man inside his head observed him dispassionately. 'This is it, Herbert,' said the little man. 'This is the grand finale, the final scene in this play, and you are the star!' Herbert remained standing quite still, and silent, and his thoughts skipped about. For years he had been living rough, belonging nowhere, an unwelcome alien in a foreign land, being rapidly despatched from one camp to another like a mislaid parcel on the railway. All those eternal bunks, all the same in every camp! The Nissen huts, the cold, the endless boiled vegetables! The smell of other people's clothing! All they had longed for was the news that they could go home! Now, here it was! And... he didn't want to go.

He was happy here! After years of being a number, issued with everything he required in the practical sense, he felt that here at least he was 'Herbert Baum-Hacker', a person in his own right. He had his own room, a bit of privacy, his own things. Although town bred, he liked farm work. True, it was very hard work, but he found that the eternal order, the inevitability of the seasonal cycle, satisfied something within him. His lessons in Geography as a schoolboy had misled him, for the Midlands had been classified as industrial, whereas this area of South Warwickshire, bordering onto the Cotswolds, was particularly lovely.

He liked and respected the Boss, and in all his dealings with him, the Boss had seen to it that Herbert had kept his personal dignity. He liked the cowman, and his kindly wife, and he had the feeling that all the people among whom he worked no longer thought of him as a German prisoner, but just 'Herbert'.

This was the first time since he had left home that he had managed to put down any roots, and to a man like Herbert, roots were important. His life had acquired some stability, and, within reason, he knew what tomorrow would bring. He had always hated the transitory. Suddenly, he felt almost cast adrift, and he knew that he could not take another uprooting, not at this stage.

The Boss went on to explain that his old firm had made an application for Herbert's return, and all the necessary formalities had now been completed. Papers were waiting for him back in the camp office. He listened to this with only half an ear, and then a voice said, "I don't want to go back" and he realised that it was his own.

It was the Boss's turn to be astonished. "You don't want to go? You mean it? You would be home in time for Christmas, you know. If everything went well."

"No!" Herbert said, and his voice was not quite steady. "I don't want to go. Not yet, anyway!"

The Boss leaned back in his chair. "Look, Herbert! Are you certain about this?" Herbert nodded, his throat seemed to have dried up a bit. "Well, if you are, I will telephone the camp and tell them. Personally, I'm very pleased that you want to stay with us, you are a damn good worker, and we should miss you, I need hardly tell you that. But... this decision must be yours and yours only. I must not influence you!"

Herbert's thoughts flew to the new cook-housekeeper. The cowman had told him that her name was Marie, and that she was very good at the job, and a damn good cook! He had seen her a few times, just passing to and fro when he went up to the garden, but he hadn't spoken to her yet, although she had smiled at him! He was working on it though! He felt himself redden slightly.

"I would like to stay longer!" he told the Boss.

He heard nothing more about this for some weeks, and then an officer and an interpreter arrived at the house, and Herbert was once again sent for.

'They are going to try and make me go back,' he thought. 'They think I'd be more use to them working over there' and he wondered if he had to do as he was ordered, or if he had any choice at all in the matter. But he needn't have worried, for this was an entirely different plan.

It was carefully explained to Herbert, via the interpreter so that there could be no misunderstanding, that all prisoners living out on farms were to be made 'temporary civilian farm workers' and they were to be paid, by the farmer, a proper weekly wage. Four pounds, ten shillings. Out of this, one pound, ten shillings would be deducted to pay for their 'keep' and the rest was cash in their hand. All this, only if he was agreeable of course. Herbert was delighted! Agree? You bet he would! Money to spend!

Real money instead of those bloody interminable cigarettes. The phrase 'wealth beyond the dreams of

212

avarice' dredged itself up from somewhere and floated across the front of his brain, but the little man inside his head was sour!

'Fool!' said the little man. 'Fool! Turning yourself into a farm labourer when you could go back home, be an engineer, take up your proper life...'

'Aw! Piss off...' Herbert silently told the little man.

Grandiose schemes, fantasies, moved in a fuzzy cloud inside Herbert's eyelids. Three whole pounds a week, just for spending money. This to someone with a cupboard full of fags, and damn all else but the occasional tip. There was just one thing; he would never again have anything else on tick! That had worried him to death, and he wouldn't fall for that one again. But then, with three whole pounds, he could easily save up and buy whatever took his fancy. What Herbert was going to accomplish with his new-found wealth was hardly worth the mention,

The four of them, Alfred, Horst, Werner and Herbert, talked the whole thing over in Herbert's quarters that evening. They had all had a similar visit, and the scheme had been fully explained to each of them. Horst and Werner were all for it, since they didn't think they would ever be able to go back to their homes, which were now in East Germany, and this was in Russian occupation.

Alfred, who had married on his last leave, and had not seen his wife since, was naturally anxious to go back home as soon as ever he could. Herbert, looking at him, felt a bit guilty really, because he had had the opportunity of going home, and had not wanted to take it, whereas poor old Alfred would have walked all the way, and swam across the channel, to get back home to his Eva, smiling brightly into the camera.

"You are a lucky man, Alfred," said Horst.

"I'd want to go back home too, if I had an Eva," said Werner.

"It can't be long now," Herbert said. "If they are making us civilians, and letting us come and go as we like, it can't be long before they send you back home."

Alfred, a little reassured, replaced the snapshot.

After weeks of the usual bureaucratic red tape, and what seemed endless form filling, the day of Herbert's civilian status eventually dawned. The Boss drove him to keep their appointment at the Camp Labour Office. The contract, already agreed, had been drawn up and was awaiting their signature, over a sixpenny stamp. The date was 5th February 1948. They signed, everybody shook hands with everybody else, Herbert was given a ration book, clothing coupons and an Alien Certificate, and… he was a civilian.

That evening, he lay on his camp bed flat on his back, his hands behind his head, and reflected upon the strange and alarming twists that life sometimes takes.

With a mere stroke of a pen, he was a civilian! There he was, living the life of any young man in a town like Hamburg, and with a stroke of a pen, he was a soldier, fighting for the Third Reich. And everything had been turned upside down. He hadn't thought about the Führer and the Third Reich for a long time, he realised, although all those years ago, he had thought about it all the time. Just now, it seemed more important to worry about the milk yield, and the fat content!

Then came the chaos of the German retreat, the shelling, the field hospital, and suddenly he was no longer a soldier, but a prisoner. He had been taken by the enemy, he owned nothing, and he was nothing, merely a number on a file. Now, with yet another stroke of probably the self same pen, he was a civilian, although still an alien, with money, ration book, everything! It's a bloody good job, he reflected, that you can't see too far into the future! If he had ever thought all this was going to happen to him, he'd have gone and hid in a cave and become a hermit.

He had already decided that the first thing he would do when he had saved up a bit of money, was to buy some clothes. At no time in the last six years had he been able to choose what he would wear. He had been issued with tunics, trousers, underwear, socks. Told when to put them on, and when to take them off! But that was all changed now, and he was to be allowed the supreme luxury of personal choice, within the range of his clothing coupons of course.

What should he get? Well, he'd have some coloured socks for a start! He glanced towards his feet. Bloody hell, he'd worn grey socks for so long he was surprised when he took them off to find that the skin beneath was still pink! He hated grey! And brown! All the drab colours he had been wearing. Some coloured socks, and perhaps a nice check jacket. He had seen a pair of wide camel coloured trousers that he really rather fancied... but he couldn't manage everything at once. He'd have to save up a bit first if he was going to have all this lot.

Then, he decided, when he was dressed in his new clothes and barbered properly, he would ask Marie if she would come out with him, perhaps to the pictures, or down to the local for a drink.

He set about saving with his customary organisation and method, added to this he received a few tips, and then thought that he could undertake his first shopping trip. Werner, who had also been saving and for the same reasons, suggested that they should go together, so that they could help each other out. They were both still a bit doubtful about travelling into the nearest town, on the local bus, and about their use of English. They also realised too, that although the war had been over for some time, there was still a little hostility in some quarters, and one or two people held firmly to the belief that the British were 'too soft' with German prisoners.

They went off together, assing about like a pair of schoolboys let off for the afternoon, and returned home hours later, loaded down to the plimsoll line with paper bags and string wrapped parcels.

The next day, Herbert presented himself in front of Marie. He was dressed in his newly acquired finery, and was, on the whole, rather pleased with himself. After years of grey and brown, he had rather gone overboard on colour (so had Werner). Herbert wore a loud check jacket, with rather a lot of red and green in it, tapering from wide padded shoulders, down to his hips. He had bought the camel coloured trousers and had pressed a crease down the front of the wide legs, so sharp that you could have cut your finger on it.

His shirt was dark red, a sort of maroon, and lime green socks were clearly visible over his new crepe soled 'correspondent' or 'brothel creeper' shoes. He cleared his throat, and said, self-consciously, "You would please like to come with me, out to the pictures?"

Marie, with great presence of mind, did not say a word about his new clothes, sensing the effort that this approach had cost him. She didn't want to hurt him, but she was not too keen on the idea of going out with him, either. She said so, quite plainly, "I don't mind coming to the pictures with you! In fact, I'd quite like it, but it's no good you trying to get too friendly, trying to make more than just that out of it. You'll be going home to Germany sooner or later, and you'll forget all about us here. It's better not to start anything... then we shan't hurt each other."

But Herbert did not give up that easily. He knew perfectly well what she meant, and he understood. There had been many foreigners in Britain during the war, of all nationalities, and having got involved with local girls, they had departed whence they came, leaving a trail of unhappiness in their wake. Herbert had no intention of doing this, and anyway, any fool could see that Marie was not the type for any casual encounter. He persisted. Marie went to the pictures with him and for a drink afterwards. And lots of times after that. This was one battle that Herbert, fighting all alone, had won, hands down.

They had a marvellous summer together; Herbert was now free to come and go as he liked, in his own time, and Marie, of course, had some time off. For years and years afterwards, whenever Herbert looked back upon the summer of 1948, through the Vaseline-smeared lens of memory, it seemed a halcyon time, a time of long sunny days, of a countryside so green, lush and filled with blossom, and of peaceful, still, sweetly scented evenings.

They went for long walks taking a packet of sandwiches to share; they borrowed a couple of ancient and unsafe bicycles, and ventured into the Cotswolds, delighting at the mellow stone villages, and rose-covered walls. They went on the river, with Marie in a flowered cotton frock, and Herbert struggling to row in a hired boat. He bought her a box of chocolates with his entire sweet ration coupons, and they shared them, tied up on the bank, beneath a willow tree. They sat on a bench in the local park, and she attempted, not very successfully, to teach him to knit.

Marie had great sensitivity, and acute observation. With her, Herbert felt completely at ease, and could be just himself. And they talked. Talked all the time, about everything under the sun. Herbert told her about his mother, his family, the house in Hamburg. But he didn't tell her much about the war, and the fighting. He would do so later, perhaps, but it did not seem very important right now, and it was an area where he was still a bit raw. Touch it roughly, or too often, and he found that it still hurt.

He had no difficulty in making himself more than understood, and not only in words. By the end of the summer his English was perfect, and he was in love with Marie.

Later that year, the British Government again showed itself magnanimous, and sent nine hundred and thirty-eight former prisoners home to Germany on a month's leave, paying the fare on condition that they returned to England to work on the land for at least a further twelve months.

Herbert had to go. He felt he must return home to see his parents and make sure that all was well with them. He knew his mother had been hurt that he had not wanted to go back when he had the opportunity, and he thought if he went back this time, he could somehow explain things to her so that she would be more likely to understand. He would tell her about Marie too, and take a photograph to show her. Circumstances had kept him apart from the family for so long now; it seemed as though their lives hardly touched at all, and they were all growing away from each other. He felt he must take this chance, now it was offered.

When he broke the news to Marie, she paled and became very quiet. He knew that she was thinking he would not come back, that once he had been home his parents would persuade him to stay with them.

"How little you know me," he said, smiling gently. He cupped her pale face in his hands, and kissed her. "But we shall have the rest of our lives to remedy that, I think!"

From his pocket, he took a sixpenny piece that he had already cut into two halves with a chisel.

"Look," he said. "What use is half a sixpence to anybody? You keep this, and when I come back, we will join the two halves together again! And I promise you, I will come back."

On December 29th 1948, the prisoners sailed from Harwich, bound for Germany. One month later, two hundred and seventy-one of them returned to this country. Herbert was among them, his half sixpence safely in his breast pocket.

EPILOGUE

After Herbert returned to England, he continued to work on the same farm, eventually finishing up as personal valet to the boss. In 1950 he changed his job, and began work as a printer's compositor. He married Marie in 1953, when he considered that he had saved up enough, and thirteen months later, their daughter was born. They still live in England.

Horst left his employment at the local mill in 1949, and became a bricklayer. He married in 1952, and still lives in this country.

Werner returned to Germany in 1959, but has now settled in Australia, working as a photo chemist. He married his German pen-friend, and they now have four children.

Alfred was able to return to his wife in 1948, and they still live in Germany where Alfred was able to carry on his old trade as a carpenter.

VERTRAG.

Zwischen dem   (farmer *Karl McConville*, wohnhaft *Kinela* (address)
(von nun ab 'Landwirt' genannt) einerseits, und dem *Arno Christiansen* (worker)
(von nun ab '.rbeiter genannt andrerseits, wurde am *Fifth*
des Monats *February* 194*8*, das Folgende vereinbart:-

1.   Der Landwirt wird den arbeiter einstell und der .rbeiter wird dem Landwirt
als landwirtschaftlicher .rbeiter auf dem Gut des Landwirts in *Kinela* dienen,
unter und gemaess den folgenden Bedingungen und Grundsaetzen:-

2.   Die Beschaeftigungsdauer ist fuer die Zeit vom *Fifth*   Tage
des Monats *February* 194*8* bis zum 31. Tag des Monats Dezember 194*8*
festgelegt, falls sie nicht vorher dadurch beendigt wird, dass eine derveiden
Parteien der anderen eine Woche Kuedigung gibt.

3.   Waehrend der Beschaeftigungsdauer wird der .rbeiter:

   (a) nicht von irgend jemand anderem als dem Landwirt oder mit anderer
        als landwirtschaftlicher .rbeit beschaeftigt werden;
   (b) zu jeder Zeit die Pflichten eines Landarbeiters sorgfaeltig, so wie
        vom Landwirt verlangt, ausfuehren;
   (c) dem Landwirt den Betrag von £ *5.0.0.* fuer die Kosten der Bekleidung,
        welche von den Militaerbehoerden zusaetzlich der Bekleidung erlaubt
        worden ist, welche normalerweise von heimgesandten deutschen
        Kriegsgefangenen nehalten werden kann, zurueckzahlen. Die
        Zurueckzahlung wird unter den Bedinführen stattfinden, die seitens der
        beiden Parteien zu Beginn des .rbeitsverhaeltniss arrangiert worden
        sind. Der Betrag wird von dem Landwirt an Stelle des arbeiters den
        .rbeiters den Militaerbehoerden bezahlt werden.

   Der Landwirt wird:-

   (a) Dem .rbeiter einen Lohn zahlen, welcher nicht weniger als den Minimal
        und Ueberstundensatz darstellt, der zur Zeit seitens des
        landwirtschaftlichen Lohnsatz-ausschusses festgelegt worden ist
        (dieser Minimalsatz betraegt zur Zeit fuer erwachsene arbeiter fuer
        eine 48 Stunden Woche *£4.0.0.*):-
   (b) als Teilzahlung des Lohnung und an stelle von Bargeld den arbeiter
        mit voller Kost und Logis versehen, seren Wert von Zeit zu Zeit durch
        einen Erlass des Landwirtschaftlichen Lohnsatz-ausschussesfestgelegt
        word (dieser Wert betraegt augenblicklich *£1.0.0.* pro Woche);

   (c) Dem .rbeiter solche bezahlten Ferien gewaehren, zu denenland-
        wirtschaftliche .rbeiter zur Zeit gesetzlich befugt sind;
   (d) den grafschaftlichen Exekutiv-ausschuss fuer Kriegs Landwirtschaft
        sofort benachrichtigen, falls eine der beiden Parteien das
        .rbeitsverhaeltnis abzubrechen befugt hat;
   (e) SONE DIESER VERTRAG UNTERZEICHNET WORDEN IST, DEN MILITAERBEHOERDEN
        £ *5.0.0.* FUER BEKLEIDUNG BEZAHLEN, die den .rbeiter zusaeglich der
        Bekleidung gegeben worden ist, die heimgeschickte Kriegsgefangene
        normalerweise behalten duerfen. Der Landwirt wird diesen Betrag von
        dem .rbeiter zurueckerhalten, gemaess den Bedingungen, die mit dem
        .rbeiter, gemaess dessen Verpflichtung unter Paragraph 3 (c) dieses
        Vertrages, vereinbart worden sind.
4.   Der Erlass des landwirtschaftlichen Lohnsatz-Ausschusses von 3. Juli 1946,
bezueglich .rbeiter ohne landwirtschaftliche Erfahrung soll nicht auf diesen
Vertrag .nwendung finden.

                                                        Landwirt
                                                        .rbeiter
Zeuge fuer die Unterschrift der beiden Parteien:
   NAME *Shaver*   .NSCHRIFT   CAMP LABOUR OFFICE
   BERUF Camp Labour Officer   ZEUGE

   Altactin 9 all   5 February 1948   Efreugton

Lightning Source UK Ltd.
Milton Keynes UK
UKHW040703010319
338259UK00001B/61/P